The Chimp *Who* Loved Me
AND OTHER SLIGHTLY NAUGHTY STORIES OF A LIFE WITH ANIMALS

By Annie Greer & Tim Vandehey

Note: The stories and examples contained in this book are based on the author's experiences and do not represent any one person, group of people or company unless expressly stated. Similarity to any one person or persons is coincidental and unintentional, so please don't sue us.

Copyright © 2010 Annie Greer and Tim Vandehey

All rights reserved. No part of this book may be used or reproduced without the written permission of the Publisher. Printed in the United States of America. For information address Diva Publishing and Broadcasting, 800 Miami Springs Drive, Longwood, Florida 32779.

Design by Tim Vandehey

www.thechimpwholovedme.com

Library of Congress Cataloging-in-Publication Data

Greer, Anne, Vandehey, Timothy S.
 The chimp who loved me: and other slightly naughty tales of a life with animals / by Annie Greer and Tim Vandehey — 1st ed.

 1. Humor—Popular works. 2. Animals—Popular works. 3. Veterinary—Popular works. Title: And other slightly naughty tales of a life with animals.

ISBN: 978-0-578-07263-0

Table of Contents

Introduction 9

PART ONE: QUIXOTIC EXOTICS

The Chimp Who Loved me 25

Animal House... 37

The Girl Who Cried Wolf 45

Spongebob Squarepans 51

Panther Bait... 55

Hump Daze 61

PART TWO: FUNNY FARM

Is That a Squirrel In Your Pants, Or Are You Just Happy To See Me? 69

Deer Diary.. 77

The Special Needs Chicken 81

All Things Sweaty and Stinky 85

Days of Swine and Roses 91

Horses and Goats and Sheep...Oh, My!.................... 99

Boyfriend Abuse 107

Kid Stuff... 113

Diva, the Special Needs Turkey.............................. 123

Hellshire Farm 129

Cattle Call 137

The Pig and the Psychic 141

The Hills Have Eyes, the Sequel 147

PART THREE: CLINICALLY INSANE

Underwear a la Carte 159
A Cloister of Monks 163
Chow, Baby 167
The Illustrated Man 171
The High Life 175
Dr. Peck 179
Our Crazy Cat Lady 183

Annie
To Mr. Piggy, Prince of Pigs, who left us on Christmas Eve 2009.
You were truly "some pig."

Tim
For Dawn, who is the music to my words.

INTRODUCTION

My day usually revolves around telling twenty-five or so employees what to do, where to go and how to get there. That, combined with shepherding a bunch of animals around the farm, can be mentally exhausting, so when a friend offered me the chance of helping out at a writers' seminar, staying for three days in a beautiful hotel, sans employees, responsibilities and animals, I thought it over for a millisecond, and screamed "Yes, oh, yes!" in a manner that I'm sure made my husband, Kent, quite jealous.

The seminar was organized by the world-famous Mark Victor Hansen, and was aimed at helping budding authors realize their publishing dreams. This was going to be the perfect opportunity to pick up some useful tips, pretend I lived a "normal life," escape the office and most relaxing of all, be told what to do, where to go, and how to get there. Yes, I know it sounds a little odd, but to have the freedom of not making any decisions was truly liberating.

The first day coincided with the launch of the new book by Hansen and Art Linkletter, *How to Make the Rest of Your Life the Best of Your Life*. After attending a lecture the devotees lined up patiently waiting their turn to be the first to buy an autographed copy. The seminar workers, such as me, sat behind the desks hidden behind stacks of the new volumes. Out of the side of my eye, I saw a potential "queue jumper," (a hanging offense in my native England), pick up a book and saunter back to his adjoining booth. Now, remember, you are dealing with someone here who has taken down a deer barehanded, so don't underestimate my speed of motion. Quick as a flash, I slammed my hand on top of the book, smiled sweetly, and said, "That'll be $29.95, please."

"Oh, I'll be right back with it. I'm just going to take a quick look at it!" the tall stranger said. "Not without $29.95 you won't," I retorted, guarding my stack of books with the intensity of a pit bull. I caught the glint of an earring in his ear, and mentally prepared myself for a good verbal scrap.

"But I wrote it!" he exclaimed. Oh ho! *We have a right one here, guv'nor,* I thought. Has he no shame? But remembering my duty of the weekend was to be polite and helpful to all attendees, I still smiled, perhaps a little less sweetly, and pointed out, that I failed to see his name on the front of the book cover. Did he think this blonde was dumb?

"I am a ghost writer and I wrote this book," he said. Well, this had me momentarily stumped. Seeing that actions were going to speak louder than words, he opened the first page, scrolled down with his finger, and there it was. An acknowledgment to Tim Vandehey for "all the help with the book." Glancing up, I immediately noticed his name badge, which clearly stated the matching name. Oh dear. I had managed to piss off a major Mark Hansen friend in the first two hours. My dreams of a peaceful, stress free weekend were being to fade rapidly.

I was relieved to find that my sparring partner seemed to find the incident slightly amusing. Battle over. A little later everyone arranged to meet for a drink in the hotel lobby. I went upstairs and in the luxury of my private room, without an animal needing food or help in sight, I prepared for a leisurely get together with everyone including Kent, who was driving down to meet me. All was well. I was really looking forward to the two of us having a good night out. I waited by the elevator patiently. Then my cell phone rang. Caller ID told me it was my daughter Becky. I flipped open the phone.

Immediately I could hear panicked screaming. Any parent will understand how the heart stands still for just a moment upon getting this type of call, and then restarts at twice the normal rate. As both kids were now driving, my first thought was that there had been a horrible accident. Trying to calm my hysterical daughter down enough to get basic information, no matter how awful, I kept telling her to take a deep breath and speak.

All I got was that someone was nearly dead. Not what I wanted to hear. "Speak to Tina," she said, passing the phone to her sister. A much calmer older daughter explained that they were okay, no one had been in an accident but our oldest cat, April, had been in the gas dryer for a while.

Well…that was okay then.

Wait. What?

My restful, peaceful feeling was rapidly slipping away. Fortunately, Tina had just completed EMT school and was a technician at our veterinary hospital. She had never hesitated, but acted with great instinct and knowledge and ended up saving one of our little cat's lives.

It turned out that my youngest had opened the dryer door, thrown in all her going-out clothes, closed the door, set the heat on high and waited at the kitchen counter for them to be ready. There came a rhythmic thumping that she thought came from her tennis shoes circulating around the dryer. She drummed in time on the kitchen counter for about ten minutes.

"Must be dry by now," she thought and flung open the dryer door. Horror! There was little April lying on her back, pouring blood from her eyes, ears and nose. She was barely alive. Screaming, Becky became helpless with shock. Tina told her to fill the sink with cold water and throw anything at all from the freezer in there, and then Tina plunged the cat into the icy water. Then she rang Kent and put an IV line into April to start fluids.

Kent met the girls at the hospital and administered every drug possible to help with brain swelling as April's internal temperature was too high to even register on the thermometer. Her pupils were two different sizes, indicating brain damage. As is so often the case, he had done all he could and now it was down to her will to live and positive thoughts and prayers.

And how was I doing? About as well as could be expected. Not only was I devastated at the thought of losing our little cat, but I knew Becky must be feeling horribly guilty. I spoke to her for a long time trying to calm her down. Eventually, she agreed to still go to see her friends and I descended in the elevator trying to compose myself before meeting my new companions.

Apparently, not very successfully. When under stress, I have a habit of running my hands through my hair, and ending up looking like Nicky from *Raising Arizona*. This was one of those times. People asked me what was up. "Nothing much," I said as casually as I could. "My cat was in the dryer on high for ten minutes, and isn't awfully well."

Horrified, the group asked what happened. One story led to another as I recalled other deaths, near deaths, births and the myriad of oddities that my life seemed to consist of. What seems everyday life to me apparently was amusing and entertaining to others.

"You should write a book about this," Tim said.

"Yeah, yeah," I said. "Everyone tells me that but I simply don't have time."

"Then let me do it for you. I am a ghost writer, remember?" he said, a twinkle in his eye as he remembered our first meeting.

And that, dear readers, is how we have come to share these stories with you. On reading them in writing for the first time, I have laughed out loud, cried some, but most of all felt a strong feeling that we were doing honor to these marvelous creatures that allowed us to share their lives, and without whom there would be no book.

What about April, the cat? As I write this, she is sitting by me, purring loudly, as always. She survived but lost most of her ears, severely burnt her feet and lost a quarter of her tail. But she is happy and outgoing. April had always been afraid of her own shadow after coming to us as an abused kitten. Now, she greets strangers with enthusiasm and really loves life.

The dryer prescription could change the world. Think about it. No need for Prozac and lobotomies, or expensive counseling and therapy. Simply, turn the gas dryer on high for ten minutes and take a spin. It could change your life. Tim has helped change my life by finally turning it into literature. My hope is that you enjoy it and laugh and cry as I have.

Annie Greer
Apopka, FL
August 2010

INTRODUCTION

I met Annie back in 2006 at one of Mark Victor Hansen's (the guy who co-created *Chicken Soup for the Soul*) Mega-Book Marketing conferences in Orlando, Florida. I had just gone through a frightening incident regarding my wife's health (which turned out fine; today she's better than ever) and needed to get away for a few days.

Annie was volunteering at one of the information tables, which really was a misnomer as no one had really told her much and she was getting by on her two staples: common sense and her bottomless fount of dry, English humor. Her mantra later in the conference would become, "I don't know, but I'll find someone who does." As Bill Bryson once wrote, she was radiant with ignorance.

We collided when I tried to abscond with a copy of the book *How to Make the Rest of Your Life the Best of Your Life*, which I had ghostwritten for Mark and the great Art Linkletter. I grabbed a copy and started to walk away, but Annie put me in a sleeper hold, which is to say, she glared at me and said, "I don't see your name on the cover."

When I showed her my name badge and then my acknowledgement in the front of the book, she got an "Uh-oh" look on her face and I think she thought she was in trouble with one of Mark's inner circle, but I'm a sucker for a woman with an English accent, and I let it go.

For the rest of the weekend, Annie and I chatted. She told me stories that became more and more incredible: her many encounters with crazy patients at the three veterinary clinics and she and her husband Kent ran north of Orlando; her diseased jawbone that resulted in a bone transplant from a cadaver, leading to the priceless quip that if she ever wrote her autobiography it would be called *Dead Man Talking*, and finally her story about being sexually assaulted in the shower by a chimpanzee.

Well, you can't slip a great story by this intrepid reporter, so after I picked myself up off the floor and wiped the laugh-tears off my face, I said, "That's it. I'm writing your book." And so a cross-country partnership was born.

Since then, this book has slowly wound its way toward completion over the last three years. We've had many false starts, including landing an agent but then never being able to find a book deal because apparently publishers want their animal books to be warm and cuddly and like *Marley and Me*. *The Chimp Who Loved Me* is largely about shit, pee, sex and death. Go figure.

I've had a second child and moved from my beloved California to the even better Bainbridge Island, Washington. Annie has endured more trials than Job, including swine flu, a mysterious disease that affected one of her daughters, a 2008 hurricane that nearly inundated the veterinary clinics, legal troubles with unhinged employees, the miscarriage of her first grandchild and the loss of her beloved mother to cancer. Through it all, she's kept her upper lip stiff, her sense of humor intact and the wine flowing, thank God.

I'm proud to finally bring her hysterically funny, nearly unbelievable and truly wonderful stories to the reading public after all this time. I'm even prouder to call her my friend.

    Tim Vandehey
    Bainbridge Island, WA
    August 2010

Author's Note:

These stories are told exclusively from Annie's point of view. Tim has served as interviewer, editor and book doctor, but he's not crazy enough to get into a cage with a pissed-off cougar or a wild wolf. So when you read "I," that's Annie talking, because she IS crazy enough to do those things, thank Heaven.

This book benefits animal charities
20% of the author profits from the sale of this book will be donated to a selection of animal-related charities around the country. We are proud to support rescue societies, shelters, service animal training centers and other organizations that help improve both the lives of animals and the humans who love them.

THE CHIMP WHO LOVED ME

**PART ONE:
QUIXOTIC EXOTICS**

CHAPTER ONE

The Chimp Who Loved Me

I remember seeing the TV show "Daktari" in the 1960s, when I moved from Africa to England. This gentle show featured a veterinarian working on a game reserve surrounded by four-legged companions like Clarence the cross-eyed lion and Judy the chimp. My school companions were convinced this must have been how I had lived on a daily basis; they didn't realize that my family came from a city that looked just like any other. But that was how I wished my life could be. I dreamed of the day when I would work alongside such creatures and share in their world.

Be careful what you wish for? Understatement.

A number of years ago, Kent had a client who provided trained animals for the entertainment industry. In an ideal world, after these animals were too old to perform, they would be relocated to preserves where they could roam free. But it is more common for star animals to fade into anonymous retirement in a sanctuary or a medical research facility. And few creatures' plights affect humans more than those of chimpanzees.

In April 2009, Cheeta, the chimp companion of Tarzan, celebrated his seventy-seventh birthday, making him the oldest chimp on record. A diabetic, he was served sugar-free birthday cake and did a spot of painting for a perfect day. When Cheeta was starring in films in 1930s, it was the first time humans were really exposed to the engaging, human-like behavior of these primates.

A love affair began that continues today. The wide grins, the slapstick actions—they came together to create a persona that fires up our maternal instincts or our desire for a goofy sidekick.

As a result, we've anthropomorphized chimps (and other primates) to a ridiculous degree. It never fails to amaze me how many people think how cute it would be to have a simian in the house. They think chimps in particular are just cuddly clowns who make faces and swing from the light fixtures all day. It would be like living with a cross between Jim Carrey and Tarzan! What fun! Honey, let's get a chimp!

This is your flight attendant speaking; time for your reality check. Chimps are manipulative, extremely aggressive beings that are about five times stronger than a grown male human. They rule by intimidation and sexual attacks in the wild. Male chimpanzees will rape females (or males) without any consideration as to relationship or familial connection. It's like living with a furry fraternity of one, the real "Animal House."

Kissing (and Other Things) Cousins
Depending on the testing methodology used by the people who spend your tax dollars to determine such things, chimps share from ninety-four percent to ninety-eight percent of our DNA. The main difference between them and us appears to be that

our extra genes allow us to use verbal language and incorporate the idea of sharing and helping.

So instead of raping, people generally beg for sex. Then again, a research project in Africa discovered that male chimps exchange meat for sex, a transaction that occurs every Saturday night at thousands of upscale steakhouses around the country. Chimpanzees also live in a male dominated society where the strongest wins and anything goes. Hmm, perhaps it's closer to ninety-eight percent after all.

Fortunately, it's not easy for the average *Animal Planet* fan to get and keep an ape. There are strict regulations and it costs a bunch of cash—about $50,000 for an infant chimp, Visa and MasterCard not accepted. But that doesn't stop some people. We have seen regulations circumvented, certificates fraudulently changed, and inspectors tricked. Be that as it may, the fact remains that many people who cheat their way to chimp parenthood get a bit more than they bargained for.

Let us say you were...an eccentric pop star with limitless wealth and a penchant for young, hairy companions (insert your own legally approved, non-plagiarized sick joke here). You decide a chimp is the must-have accessory of the season. Initially, the chimp will be clutched to your chest, baby fashion, and you will cart this bundle of wide-eyed joy everywhere, 24/7.

I can tell you from personal experience that looking into the deep brown, twinkling eyes of a baby chimpanzee instantly freezes all logical brain function. Sentiment takes over as you reach out to hold your ancient ancestor. It doesn't take much to become completely hooked. Before you know it, you're ready to buy formula bottles and a copy of *What to Expect When You're Expecting an Ape.*

Oh, did I forget to mention the cage? You'll need one. Government specifications are very stringent, requiring incredibly thick gauge wire, lots of room and environmental stimulation. Be prepared to fork over another $10,000. There's a reason for this. Not only are chimps incredibly strong, but smart and aggressive, too. Over time, as your baby chimp matures, he will start to work his way up your family's social totem pole with surprising ease.

Do not be fooled by his apparent love for you. Chimps are highly intelligent and they have a knack for seeing anybody's weak points and zeroing in on them like a missile. Your furry little baby wants to dominate your household, defile your women, and send you packing. Trust me on this.

Swingin' Sammy
Kent and I don't advertise that we work with exotic animals, but we're the ones people call when their jaguar is in labor or their tapir has an impacted wisdom tooth.

Our last task before we flew to Las Vegas for a holiday in the summer of 2008 was to vaccinate 15 tigers. We know our way around these unpredictable, incredible creatures, so we try to help out. Part of our job when caring for exotics is to act as nursemaids when they're sick. I have babysat lions, tigers and more, all very happily. Let me tell you: apes are a different ball of fur.

Chimpanzees can catch illnesses such as colds from humans. When the owners of Sammy, a nine-month-old male chimp, had to take an urgent trip out of town, they left him in our care because he was suffering from a head cold. I was thrilled to have this opportunity to babysit for the weekend; I had known Sammy since his birth and helped with his raising and feeding for short intervals.

Chimps spend much of their early infancy clinging to their mothers, breastfeeding to the age of four, so surrogate mother is a full-time job. One of the hardest things to train a chimp to do is abandon its instincts and leave its mother. Sammy's new full-time mommy was tall, blonde and a former model. I'm no model, but I'm blonde and figured I'd be an acceptable stand-in.

When Rick and Jen came to the door, they were loaded with enough baby clothes, diapers, toys, swings, food, bottles, etc. for a month. I wondered if I would be watching one chimp or the population of Sesame Street. There were cute little bottles with bunnies running around the sides, tiny shorts from the Gap, those fluffy little blankies for cuddling at night, a special lambkin to hold tight...even the diapers seemed adorable at that point.

Then came Sammy. *Adorable Sammy.* With a little coaxing (and prying his pinching fingers off his mommy's arms) he finally reached for me, grabbed one of my boobs and stared up into my eyes, which were watering, not so much from the emotion of the moment as from the pressure of his pincer-like hand on my mammary gland. However, what I call the Chimpanzee Vortex took over: all pain vanished as Sammy's soft brown eyes looked trustingly into mine. It was love at first sight. His black spiky hair stood up around his head like a shock of hay; I couldn't resist running my hand through the four inches of black silk that covered his little body. The skin around his mouth was soft and pink, but he had an endearing little whiskery beard.

I felt at one with nature. We had bonded in a special moment of maternal bliss. As Rick and Jen waved goodbye I held Sammy in my arms, gave him a cuddle and missed having babies in the house. He weighed about twelve pounds and was bundled in his blanket like a hairy papoose. This was going to be fun. What a wonder. What a treat.

What a delusional load of chimp shit.

Kent's Dominance Two-Step
If you're a grandparent, you know. Everything that seemed a chore with your own kids takes on a newness when the kids

are someone else's. My "Daktari" dream was coming true as I watched Sammy nurse from his first bottle of milk. "Wow," I thought. "It can't get better than this."

I changed Sammy's diaper (the old skills came back in a flash and I felt like Super Mom), and with order restored and a clean-smelling cutie clinging to my chest, I settled down to watch some TV with my husband. We looked like the perfect family with a new baby in the house. Kent and I had married at a point in our lives when more children were not an option, so we allowed ourselves a little daydream with Sammy as our special kid. Chimps don't care about TV as a rule; Sammy was far more interested in watching Kent's every move.

In the wild, chimpanzees rely on their perception of facial expressions to help interpret situations. Sammy fixed his brown eyes in Kent's direction. Like most men, when watching TV Kent was unable to multitask, so he was unaware of what was going on next to him. I could feel Sammy's little body tense and the hair all over his body rise into hackles, but I put it down to his unease at being in strange surroundings. Then without thinking, Kent absentmindedly draped his arm over the back of the sofa and touched my shoulders. Sammy went nuts. *Demonic Sammy*. Puffing up his hair like a horror movie character and seeming to double in size, he started to scream and bite my husband!

Figures. The one time in my life I have two men fighting over me and one of them is not only much too hairy for my taste, but he's trying to maim my life partner.

Clinging protectively to my shoulders, Sammy was jumping up and down, hooting loudly. He opened his mouth to reveal a row of gleaming teeth, each one capable of taking a chunk out of you. I remembered the case in California where two sanctuary chimps driven wild by jealousy had basically ripped apart and nearly killed a man. I didn't want my weekend of mommyhood to end in the ER.

Kent is a firm believer in the power of the pen over the sword, but he knew the situation called for a more Neanderthal approach. This was man over beast. The man who'd kissed me on our wedding day began jumping up and down, hooting loudly himself. His mouth pulled open to show a row of gleaming white teeth, each one capable of taking a healthy chunk out of a medium-rare filet mignon. He waved his arms above his head in a threatening posture; wild, primeval sounds issued from his throat. Gosh! I'd never realized my hubby could be that scary.

Sammy clearly agreed. His hair flattened back against his skin and he made cute little grunty sounds. He stretched the back of his hand out towards Kent in a conciliatory gesture. Wow, I thought. Kent really did want me for his wife! What a display of manhood! The dominance tactic worked; Sammy immediately became a compliant, submissive bundle of babyhood. Unfortunately, at this point it dawned on me that Sammy considered me not so much mommy material but potential mating material. Chimps do not sexually mature until they are around ten years old, but like teenagers, that does not stop them from experimenting before they're ready.

Thank God For Shiny Objects
Shaken but undeterred, I saw Kent off to work the next morning. I decided that since Sammy seemed calm—he was playing with some children's toys on the floor—I could take a shower. Let's recap: I was alone in the house with a powerful male animal that saw me as a possible concubine, and I was about to be naked. Not one of my brighter moments, but I digress.

I started to undress by the shower door. Then I felt eyes on me. Sammy was watching me from the doorway. Hmm. Odd, but not threatening. I stepped into the shower and turned the hot water on. Chimps do not like water, so I figured

I was safe, and I needed a little breather from carrying him all the time. Suddenly, I noticed my chimp child was gone, along with all the clothes and towels I had laid down on the floor. Suddenly, Sammy came full speed around the corner, hooting and grinning, and launched himself at me! *Fully Erect Sammy!*

All I could think was, "Oh God! I'm going to be sexually assaulted by a chimp!" I pictured the 911 call. I saw the operator laughing so uncontrollably that she forgot to send help. I tried to peel Sammy's pinching, prying hands off my naked, wet body and realized that I had to get some clothes on.

I feel that a brief aside is in order at this point. Being attacked by a chimpanzee, despite my humorous circumstances, is no laughing matter. I am constantly amazed at idiots who, despite all the evidence that chimps are savage, randy, powerful little beasts (even as a juvenile, Sammy was probably my match in strength), persist in treating them like great cuddly wuddly little babies with five o'clock shadow.

These are wild animals that should be treated with cautious respect, NOT as though they were human beings. Nothing illustrates that better than the terrible 2009 incident in which a chimp named Travis attacked and horribly mutilated a woman in Connecticut. The chimp's owners, who I will charitably call deluded, had socialized the animal to the point where he was basically their surrogate son. Travis would water the plants, ate at the table and drank wine from a glass, used the computer and even slept with the couple.

When Travis went berserk on February 16, he tore the owner's friend, Charla Nash, to pieces, despite the fact that the owner *hit him with a shovel and stabbed him with a butcher knife.* It was like that bit in *Blazing Saddles* where Gene Wilder tells Cleavon Little's sheriff, who is getting his pistol ready to shoot the hulking Mongo, "Don't shoot him. If you shoot him, you'll just make him mad." It took multiple gunshots at close range to finally take Travis down. It was a tragedy that ought never to have happened, and would not have happened if people didn't turn chimpanzees into fetishes and treated them like the beautiful, wild and potentially dangerous creatures they are. Okay, rant over.

The strength and savagery of the mating chimp were quite on my mind as I exited the shower with Sammy attached. Making what I thought were soothing, calming little hoots and grunts, I worked my way slowly towards the bedroom closet. This took ten minutes; Sammy seemed to sense that my intentions were not the same as his. I grabbed some clothes, and then I remembered that his favorite playthings were handbags with goodies in them.

Snatching anything I could find that was shiny and chimp-proof, I shoved it all in two purses. We sat on the bed together (me stark naked and dripping wet) like a couple of nervous virgins on their wedding night. I tried to remain nonchalant. Chimps are deeply suspicious beings and they pick up on any vibes that suggest danger or change. Slowly, Sammy let go of me with one hand and dug into the bag. I tried to put a shirt on—not a chance. My new boyfriend knew I was up to something. We continued in this fashion for an hour and a half. I prayed that someone would come to the door. Then I prayed they wouldn't. What in hell would I say?

Eventually, Sammy lost interest and his attention shifted to the cat that had been unfortunate enough to walk into the room. With a scream of delight he chased the kitty into the rest of the house. Men who claim that women take forever to get dressed didn't see me that morning.

Sammy the Superstar
Thanks to a chimp cage we spent a relatively peaceful night, although my illusions of becoming the next Jane Goodall were history. After breakfast, we decided to give Sammy some

fresh air by taking him to a piece of property we were developing, which would become our farm. I rode in the back of the car with him strapped into his baby seat. He was very sweet, patting my face and playing with the baby toys. The only difference at that point between him and a human baby was that he never once said, "Are we there yet?"

Sammy clung to me as we walked our forty acres of woodland and pasture. We had not really met our neighbors and were pleased to see someone working in the adjacent yard. "Hello!" Kent cried. In this part of the country, you fend off potential shotgun blasts by clearly stating your friendly intentions. "I'm Kent, this is my wife Annie and our son Sammy." Ever the comedian. The gentleman never batted an eyelid, but just waved at both Sammy and me. Apparently, we fit right in with the locals.

On the other side of the reaction scale, we take you to Tampa, Florida. Rick and Jen had returned for their chimp and we all travelled to Tampa for a conference. However, our beautiful hotel recoiled in horror at the idea of accommodating a chimp. Quick-thinking Rick pretended to be deaf; he wrote down that the chimp was his assistance animal. And the hotel staff bought this absurd, transparent lie! So Sammy had his own cot assembled in Rick and Jen's room.

We were hungry and decided to take a trip to Ybor City, a recently renovated area of Tampa famous for its Cuban influence and cigar making. The streets were packed with tourists, trendy restaurants and beautiful people. It was here that I learned the true meaning of the phrase "babe magnet." I have never seen any creature have such an effect on so many as Sammy had on that stylish throng. We were followed like the Pied Piper of Hamlin. The crowds became so large that the local police accompanied us. We were all part of Sammy's entourage.

Star power speaks, we discovered. Attempting to dine at a highly recommended restaurant, we were disappointed to learn that not a single table was to be had...until management spotted Sammy! Magically, the best table appeared. The chef even made a personal appearance at the table to find out what the young ape would like to eat. Salad was always a good choice, but I have to state jealously that I have never before had such a beautifully presented dish brought to my table. Sammy's radishes were sculpted into roses; every cucumber had been delicately peeled. It was a work of art. Every waitress in the place found an excuse to stop by to ensure we had everything we needed. Every patron discovered an urgent need to use the restroom and pass by the table. No Hollywood movie star had ever enjoyed so much attention and admiration.

Sammy, in turn, worked the crowd like a rock star. He zeroed in on the women like a fly to treacle. They were putty in his hands. His secret? Just allowing people to come close to a living myth that had been created in movies. Everyone thought they knew how a chimp would be up close: cute, cuddly, comical, and irresistible.

Sure, I thought. Just try taking a bath with the little demon in the house.

CHAPTER TWO

Animal House

One of the first books I ever read was *Born Free*, which deceived me and many others into thinking that you could raise a lion on milk and it would become a fluffy, 300-pound lap dog. Nonsense. For several years, Kent and I cared for various lion and tiger cubs for preserves and the like. They had all been raised on milk and milk alone, but the day they smelled animal blood was the day everything changed. These are the most perfect predators nature has ever created; you're not going to turn them into latte-sipping vegetarians no matter how hard you try.

Still, how many people fantasize about having a cuddly cub at home like in *The Little White Horse*, a Victorian novel by Elizabeth Goudge? Plenty, I'm sure, and they are all out of their bloody minds. All the books I read made lions sound like pretty laid-back guys as long as they were part of the family. Bullshit. The only time a lion is cute and cuddly is while it's still small enough for you to strangle it with your bare hands.

After that, it's sizing you up: "Hmm, how big a chunk could I rip out of her ass before she got really mad? Two pounds?"

We had a client who had worked with big cats and needed a vet to look after them while he was setting up another business venture. He just walked in the clinic one day and asked Kent to take a look at his tiger cub. It's really amazing, the effect that exotic animals—especially big cats—have on people, including myself. I think it's the incredible beauty combined with the fact that when you hold a baby lion or tiger, you are dancing with death. This is a creature that in a year will be strong enough to kill you without even breaking a sweat and more than willing to do so no matter how much you think it loves you. Stephen King once described cats as the "amoral gunslingers of the animal kingdom" and that's dead-on.

This gent's cat was a ten-day-old Siberian tiger named Tonya. She didn't look very good. If the cats are going to be working with humans, the breeders take the cubs away from their mothers very early so that they have a bonding experience with humans. It's a 24-hour a day job to acclimate them to man, and sometimes very hard on the cats' health. So Tonya arrived and was not in very good condition. She was missing certain vitamins. This fellow asked us to take her home and care for her, and like fools (again, there's that pattern where "Yes" escapes my mouth before my shoe can find its way in). So several cubs came home with us. That's where the big adventures began.

A Tiger In Your Toilet Tank
First of all, tiger babies don't go to the bathroom on their own (unlike human babies who don't seem to have any problem doing this, especially in the middle of the night or when you're trying to have a nice quiet dinner for a change—but I digress). Mother tigers actually lick the cubs' privates to stimulate them

to urinate and defecate. If they don't go, they can die. That's one reason a tiger has a rough tongue with bristles strong enough to strip hair off a corpse. There's a bit of trivia for your next party!

It goes without saying that I wasn't about to lick anybody's privates (insert your own joke here, you perverted bastard), but it did fall to me to massage and use warm cloths to stimulate the tigers to go to the bathroom. I also had to feed them a bottle, just like a baby's bottle, every four hours. They grip onto you with 10 little talons that are amazingly large and painful. I just sucked it up, and so did they. Still, it was wonderful. Originally I was drawn to lions, which are the most anti-social of the big cats. This was probably because of my *Born Free* experience and thoughts of Elsa. But now, after eight tiger encounters, I'm totally enamored of the striped cats.

Not that they were without their challenges. For instance, the first night you have them home, you think naively that they're going to sleep in their crate. Foolish human. Like all babies, they're not going to stay where you put them if they can help it. Tonya, our sickly female, came into our bedroom and slept in our dog's bed. And just like a baby, you're so attuned to them being awake that if they make a peep, you're awake. That first night, I remember waking up about 2 a.m. when Tonya made a noise. The entire wall of the bedroom was mirrored, and in the dark we could see that she was wide-awake and playing with her reflection. Kent and I just sat silently and watched. It was one of the most charming things I've ever seen, this tiny cub playing like a kitten in the moonlight. That first experience with Tonya was one of the easiest we've ever had.

On the other hand, can you imagine being the family dog in our house? You walk in from the yard after a good session of digging, crapping and having a good roll in some fresh horseshit and you see a cage in the middle of the floor.

Worse, you smell an animal scent you don't recognize. Your doggie mind thinks, "Oh God, not another one! What is it this time, a panda? A wombat? A fucking crocodile?"

Our dog at this time was named Candy, and she was incredible. She would mother every exotic animal that stayed with us, but not like you'd expect. Rather than following the babies around, she was a combination of ethics officer and Mother Superior at a Catholic girls' school. The young animals learned within a day that if they wanted to be near Candy, they had to remain quiet, not be pesky, and there was no playing. Candy's attitude was, "I will allow you to lie next to me."

Now, this was a 35-pound dog and she would do this regardless of the species. As her "babies" grew to weigh 100 pounds or more, they would still grovel to be near her and do whatever they had to do to avoid her disapproving growl. She was the disciplinarian of the house and she kept the creatures in line with little more than a stare and an attitude.

Bear Facts

Life with a tiger: picture a 75-pound kitten bouncing around the house—who, by the way, came with the biggest kitty litter box I've ever seen. It was the size of a small dining room table and it took a quarter-ton of kitty litter to fill it. Unfortunately, Tonya produced turds of the same relative size. It was really interesting for us to see her use that box. I swear you could hear a *thud* when those powerful feline bowels finally moved. Shovels were in order.

Of course, if you were a guinea pig or a rabbit in the house at that time, the whole thing was not so funny. The odds of being squashed flat by a massive feline paw (even at that age they're the size of tea saucers and get to the size of dinner platters) were only exceeded by the chance of being devoured during a bout of "playfulness." Of course we had Candy, the ethics officer, in the house. And, she did her job keeping order very well. There were few casualties.

Unfortunately for my children, one of the tiger's favorite games was to lie on the sofa with her ears flattened (normally they have pointy ears). Her eyes would be level with the top of the sofa and she would wait for one of the children to walk by so she could pounce on them! They were constantly being brought to the ground by this oversized kitty. It really wasn't a problem because you teach them very early on that biting isn't acceptable. You have to be vigilant and make sure it doesn't happen. The danger is not as great as you might initially think. It is amazing how easily kids adapt. Christina was ten years old and Becky was seven, so she probably got the worst of it. But both kids survived, and how many children can say they've been hunted by a tiger in their living room?

The other two characters in the house were the bears. I'd never been exposed to bears nor had I particularly wanted one. Of course I had a teddy bear as a kid, but never thought I needed to cuddle with the real thing. Bears have a reputation for being smart, stinky, unbelievably strong and endlessly, incredibly hungry. So of course it was inevitable that a bear or two would find its way into our home. God definitely has a sense of humor.

Our first bear was a male cinnamon brown bear named Kody. When he arrived…oh my God. He was the cutest little teddy bear I'd ever seen! Of all the exotics, bears need the most mothering. In the wild, they're with their mothers for about two years before she leaves them to fend for themselves. So the young bear is dependent and clingy.

There are lots of expressions having to do with bears. Some of my favorites include, "Mad as a bear with a sore head," "Hungry as a bear," and "Bad-tempered as a bear." After a few weeks with Kody, I quickly figured out why these sayings have stuck: *they're all true!* He would wake up hungry. I mean an eight-months-pregnant, "I want food NOW!" kind of hungry. Then he would immediately start screaming.

What's more, bears drink phenomenal amounts at a time. He was taking three baby bottles per feeding—milk formula mixed with cereal. I would have to premix his food because he didn't have the patience to wait while I was fiddle-faddling around mixing powdered formula and such. It had to be premixed and in the refrigerator or there was ursine hell to pay. Unfortunately he still had to wait while I heated it up in the microwave for all of 45 seconds, and bears don't have time for that crap. They want food like an addict wants crack, only with greater urgency.

When we got two bears—apparently, I was doing such a good job that I *must* have needed another one—the second one was a female. Now it was six bottles. Now I had two bears bellowing for food at the same time, six bottles, and only one pair of hands. You do the math. Hence, Christina became Victim Sorry Helper #2 (remember, that my poor child was only 10 years old). Feedings would occur at the ungodly hour of 6 a.m. If I had wanted to get up that early, I would have joined the goddamned military.

It would go this way: I'd bark at Christina like a drill sergeant, "I'm taking the brown bear. You get the black bear." We'd be dressed in our nightgowns trying to get formula heated up and the tops of the bottles back on in the zillionth of a second that the spoiled-rotten bears were willing to wait for their sustenance. The little shits would bite us on the back of the legs and start yelling if we took a nanosecond too long—and we *always* took too long. I think after a while strangers who saw me in public must have thought Kent and I were playing some sort of weird sex games because of all the cuts and bruises on my legs. If only...

So Christina and I would be literally running around the house with the bears chasing us during the time it took to microwave the bottles. The microwave would ding and I'd yell, "There's yours, Christina! Go!" Remember, the bears drink three bottles per feeding so it was three rounds of this chaos. That's a hell of a way for a fifth grader to start her day before getting ready for school.

The other things is, after young bears have eaten they usually like to suck on their mother's paw for 45 minutes. The suckling motion soothes them like a pacifier. Well, they do the same with humans—usually sucking on the inside of the arm but sometimes on the neck, which of course produces the biggest hickeys this side of Inspiration Point. I started wearing scarves everywhere, even to the grocery store. Otherwise, you know everyone's looking. What do you say? "It was a bear. Really. Not my husband. A bear." After a while, I was afraid folks would start asking me to their "swinger" parties. They probably already assumed the name of our farm was Funny.

The Bear Lady

Kody, the brown bear, enjoyed watching TV, especially the 10 o'clock news. It was very strange. He would come into the bedroom and get into bed with us. Kent would be in bed already watching TV, and Kody would sit up next to him with his fuzzy legs stuck out in front like a giant teddy bear. One night I went out to do something in the kitchen and I came back in to find Kent asleep and snoring—and the bear next to him on my pillow, in the same position, snoring just as loudly. I don't know why I didn't get my camera. All I could think was, "Great. Where do I sleep?"

As far as I know I'm the only person in the U.S. to have housebroken two bears. That was out of sheer necessity. Bear poop is not the best substance to have in your life, nor is it appreciated by the neighbors. At the time, we actually lived in a housing development, and while I don't think there were specific rules for no bears, tigers, or lions, Kent and I felt that if the homeowners' association was anal retentive about the length of the palm fronds and specks of mildew growing where the sprinklers hit the house, a bear and his poop were likely to be frowned upon, to put it mildly.

It got so that I had to take Kody out incognito. I would take him for early morning walks around the golf course, and when I heard a cyclist or runner coming, I tucked his head between my legs. They just thought the fluffy body was just part of a chow puppy. That worked…for a short while. Bears grow very big very fast, and when they do, having them in the house is no longer an option.

It's sad, really. You bond so quickly to these animals, disruptive as they can be. And it wasn't just me; the girls became so attached to the bears, tigers and other exotics. I used to take Kody to schools. Can you imagine how popular I was at my kids' school?

One of the funniest things that ever happened in that regard was when I went into McDonald's to order something and a little boy saw me and started pointing at me and shouting, "Mom, there's the bear lady!" I could see his mother's eyes get wide and then narrow; I'm sure she was thinking that *bear* was spelled "bare." So I heard myself saying, "No, no! Listen. I'm the bear lady, not the bare lady. I brought a bear to your son's school." I think she got it, but she still pulled her son away into the next line for his Happy Meal. But on the whole I still prefer the "Bear/Bare Lady" to "that dominatrix with the scratched-up legs and the hickeys on her neck."

CHAPTER THREE

The Girl Who Cried Wolf

I love wolves and their spirituality. There's something about them that is so noble and primal and intelligent—you can really see why the Native Americans worshipped them. I'm very connected to the spiritual side of animals, so when we had this opportunity to have wolves in our house, I jumped at the chance. As always, I landed in a pile of shit.

Three wolves were coming in, and initially I took in all three cubs for one night. But we soon found out that this wasn't going to be a long-term operational plan, because wolves have a peculiar odor. They have a scent gland at the base of their tails and the smell is unspeakably rank—not at all like a dog, if that's what you were thinking of. This is not like your randy beagle rubbing its butt on the living room carpet. Instead, imagine the stench of 100 wildebeest in heat sexing down their partners...on your living room carpet. That's what wolf mojo is like.

Structurally, wolves are very different from dogs, too. They have the jaw strength to snap the femur of an elk, producing 1500 pounds of bite pressure per square inch. Their diet is also nothing like a dog's. When they're babies, you bond with them not by feeding them milk but by giving them raw meat. You simply can't put this perfectly engineered hunting and killing machine into a domestic setting and assume that it will behave like Lassie. There's a reason they eat raw meat: it's the closest thing to a kill. They're gorgeous animals and marvelously spiritual creatures, but as with any wild thing, you mustn't delude yourself that this is a warm, fuzzy buddy.

We ended up keeping one of these wolves for quite a long time, and I learned that in no way are they like domestic dogs. Once, I reached in his crate while I was feeding him and he got his jaws on of one of my fingers by mistake. Now, your instinct is to pull back quickly, but the second that I began to do that, it was like being cut by a guillotine, which flayed the skin from my finger and left blood dripping down my hand. There wasn't much pain, but I know that I had to wait for the wolf to let me go (which he eventually did) or I would likely lose my finger. That was a wake-up call. Even at eight weeks, their teeth are deadly sharp.

Romeo and Juliet
The wolf we kept for a while was a magnificent animal, black with yellow eyes. At the same time, I had a tiger cub, and both were effectively disciplined by Candy the dog. That meant that for once, I had the fun part. No severing of testicles or cleaning of anal glands or cleaning out pens of hip-deep poop for this girl—at least, not this time. I got to watch the tiger and the wolf play. Understand that you'd never see this pair together in the wild. In India, the tiger and wolf are mortal enemies, yet we had them playing together constantly. It's a natural mammal instinct. All young things like to play.

There's a song in the musical *South Pacific* called, "You Have to Be Carefully Taught," about learning to hate people who aren't like you. One line from it goes, "You've got to be taught before it's too late, before you are six or seven or eight..." That's true for us and for animals, too. These two were from the Montagues and Capulets of the wild kingdom, yet they went at it like eight-year-old boys on the first day of summer break. They hadn't learned to see each other as foes, so they were friends. It was incredible to watch them "play-fight" together. We always wondered, who would win this time? It was the power of the tiger's jaws and claws vs. the quickness and agility of the wolf. Every day the results were different, but there wasn't a day that I didn't marvel at what could happen when you threw two creatures together in an environment where they felt safe and let them be babies.

Reminders

The wolf also used to go to schools with me. I got very involved in Defenders of Wildlife, who were at that time reintroducing wolves into the wild in the Rocky Mountain West. It was a controversial project, and plenty of people without the slightest understanding of wolves began screaming that the wolves would eat their livestock and kill their children. So I took my wolf out as part of a PR offensive to educate the public.

The fact is, wolves don't deserve the bad press they get. Yes, they have been known to kill livestock, but they were living on the land long before we got there, and they are alpha predators with an important role in controlling the population of grazing animals like deer and elk. When you get to know wolves and observe them up close, you see what extraordinary creatures they really are. They have an incredible social system. Young uncles take babies from their mother to rough play for a few hours so she can nap. Where the hell are the uncles in the human world when the new mom just wants to have a bath and maybe catch a Tivo'd episode of *American Idol*, huh?

Anyway, the alpha couple in the pack is the only one allowed to mate and have babies. When cubs are born, there is a joyous celebratory howling. When one dies, there is tremendous grieving. It's the omega wolf, the one on the bottom of the pack hierarchy, who brings the pack out of its grief by being a clown. This wolf will do things like taking a stick and throwing it up in the air. He's the jester, a tradition that goes back to *King Lear* and far beyond. When he has filled his purpose, he reverts back to his low place in the pack.

Wolves are naturally very shy—their first impulse is to get away from man—so it was very rare for the schoolchildren to actually see a wolf. But the kids at the schools I visited got to see this spectacular wolf with bright yellow eyes and a black coat. That was wonderful for them, but the time came when he simply got too big for such trips to be safe. Even I need the occasional reminder that these gorgeous animals, which I love to think love and trust me, are still wild predators that could slaughter me in seconds if they chose to. Part of being responsible with living creatures is knowing when they are too big or potentially dangerous to be in a family setting.

I got two reminders of that uneasy fact with this wolf. One day at work, I had taken him for an early morning run by the river. We came back to the clinic and sat on the scales on the floor so I could weigh him. By then he was taller than I was when he stood up and put his paws on my shoulders. His muzzle was at eye level, and that's a lot of teeth. Imagine what Red Riding Hood must have seen just before she slid down the Big Bad Wolf's gullet and you might have some idea.

So at this point, I was tired and sitting on the scales and without any warning at all, this giant wolf came over and very deliberately put his whole mouth on my throat. A lot of things went through my mind in that second, the foremost of which was including, "Oh shit. This isn't good. This is going to be messy." Then came the real puzzlement: "What is he doing?"

Suddenly, as quickly as he grabbed me, he let go and sat there panting as if nothing had happened. He looked for all the world like a guy who "accidentally" slid his hand down to his date's breast at the movies and then tried to pretend it wasn't intentional. It was like he forgot for a moment that I wasn't a play toy. Wolves' canines can get two or three inches long, so it's always valuable to get a reminder that they are still wild animals. I was lucky that this was, at worst, a dress rehearsal for killing and devouring me.

My second reminder came when I took him to an area where I could take him off leash (said leash, by the way, was a heavy-gauge chain). At some point in their time in a domestic setting, every wolf will challenge you to see who is the alpha; my day came when I took him to this fully fenced area. I had the kids and my mother from London with me, and a small dog, Lucy, who we still have. I have a picture of the wolf carrying Lucy around in his mouth; she looks like a dead rabbit. He would never dare do that with Candy the Great and Terrible.

I could see him running in the distance, and I whistled for him. He started coming and suddenly stopped. He glared at me from a few dozen yards away like a bull thinking of the best way to trample a matador. It was the silent, terrifying stare of a predator before it charges. I remember thinking, "It's time." I didn't know what would happen, but I knew two things: one, I'd have to concentrate more than I've ever concentrated before, and two, I needed everyone out of the field. So I told my mom, "I need you to get the kids out of here and no matter what happens, don't come in." That's not what a mother wants to hear, but she complied and got herself and the kids outside the fence.

I looked back at the wolf. He was just staring at me. Suddenly he set off toward me—fast. I can remember thinking, "I've got to stay on my feet." I'd seen a documentary about this. If you go down, you're done, even in play. This 100-pound mass of black death charged at me and hit me full in the shoulders like a linebacker trying to sack the quarterback. I had one foot braced behind the other, and somehow I stayed upright.

He bounced off me, his tongue fell off to the side of his mouth…and suddenly he looked no different than a golden retriever greeting its master when he comes home from work. To the sneaky little shit, the whole thing was just a big giggle.

That was the day I realized that he was maturing and I needed to have my guard up. Unfortunately, after that, things spiraled downhill. Even though he was technically my wolf, he ended up being taken away. He bit several people and it got to the point that no one could release him from his cage. That's when I finally realized that these animals were just commodities to many humans, kept around only as long as they were cuddly to have pictures taken with, and then sent away, abandoned, or disposed of. I just wasn't prepared for that, and that marked the end of my innocence as a keeper and surrogate mommy to exotic animals.

CHAPTER FOUR

Spongebob Squarepans

You know, I have never been lucky when it comes to winning things, like the lottery or games of chance. I did win a statue of Jesus when I was eight years old by choosing the number 11. I've been choosing 11 ever since and never had a bit of damn luck with it. Superstitions are hard habits to break.

Once, we went to a home exposition where I entered a contest: if you won the prize, a chef would come to your home and cook for you and ten of your friends. I'm a big fan of The Food Network and I imagined The Barefoot Contessa or someone of that caliber coming into my house. But no one could've been more surprised than I when I got the call that I'd won the Grand Prize. "Send out your invitations," the person on the other end of the phone said. "Give us the date for when the chef will be coming to cook for you."

How fabulous is that? I was so excited that I was on the phone with my nearest and dearest talking up the big night. We even invited the owners of Sammy, my favorite sexually molesting chimpanzee; they got a babysitter for the kids but had to bring the chimp along for the evening.

This was fine, because Sammy's best friend was my dog, Lucy. They had sibling-like relationship. Sometimes, Sammy would love and hold Lucy like she was his baby. Other times they would fight or chase each other. By now most of our friends were used to having something extraordinary at the table, so a chimp chasing a dog around the room didn't raise any eyebrows.

Anyway, the chef arrived, and I with an all-too-familiar feeling of "Oh fuck, Annie, you've stepped in it again," I realized that this was not quite The Barefoot Contessa coming to my door. This was a salesman who was selling pots and pans at the extraordinary price of $1,500 a set. How embarrassing! Now I got to entertain my guests while looking like an idiot because I genuinely thought I had won something, when even someone who had been in frozen stasis since the time of Dickens would have seen that "contest" and thought, "This is a scam to get in my house and harass my closest friends."

Undaunted, the peppy gentleman with the cookware took over my large kitchen and started to cook. He was using these pans made out of some special alloy that supposedly cut cooking time in half. The idea was that your guests would not so much be getting a crepe suzette at the table as getting a cooking demonstration live in your kitchen. I cringed as the man started his sales pitch even while he was crushing and mincing garlic, leafing lettuce and browning onions.

My guests were gracious enough not to make a big deal of it, but he was doing the whole spiel, like something out of an Erma Bombeck book: "You're going to time me starting...NOW! I'm going to show you how to cook this chicken in ten minutes!" He was going to use all four burners. Here was the catch: I have an electric range, so because you can't see a flame, it's not obvious right away whether a burner is working or not. I knew that only two worked. But I didn't know how to tell Spongebob Squarepans this. I knew it didn't matter how good those pots and pans were—without heat, he wasn't going to be doing anything but stirring and chopping and eventually scratching his head and swearing, as so many who come to my humble abode eventually do.

What I find astonishing is that I know just what to do when faced with a sexually aroused chimpanzee or a charging wolf, but I freeze like a homeless person in January when faced with telling a well-meaning man that part of my kitchen is on the fritz.

I didn't know what to do. This poor chef was probably thrilled to have a nice audience and a chimpanzee to boot. I was about to say something when Sammy and Lucy got into a sibling spat. Sammy began lobbing little donuts through the crowd, aiming for the dog. We were getting a saucepan demonstration that wasn't going to yield anything edible, with flying donuts for appetizers. Suddenly, Lucy ran around the corner, came up behind Sammy and pulled his diaper down like the Coppertone baby. Sammy grabbed one of the man's $500 frying pans and went after the dog with it. It was like a horrible nightmare come to pass.

Meanwhile, our intrepid chef was baffled as to why the chicken wasn't cooking. "It's never taken longer than ten minutes, I don't understand!" he wailed, truly distressed. I finally fessed up about the broken burners. Meanwhile, everyone was pitching in trying to calm down the animals while laughing themselves hysterical. In the end, we gave up on the food and settled on the sofa. The salesman was still trying to sell at least one $1,500 set of pots and pan, but it is very difficult do a presentation when you have a chimp as your "lovely assistant." Sammy, he of the impeccable comic timing, would come up behind the chef and clap his hands over the man's eyes, or get two pans and just start banging them together. This was not the fun gourmet party I'd envisioned, and I'm sure it wasn't how the salesman thought it would go either.

    By evening's end, the only order that poor man took came from Kent, because we both felt so bad. Oh, and half the people got food poisoning from the undercooked chicken. That was the last time I won something. You can understand why my nickname isn't "Lucky."

CHAPTER FIVE

Panther Bait

Exotic animals really are a very small component of our business down here in Animal Central, but they make up a lot of the stories because their behavior is just so fascinating...and occasionally, dangerous. Most people don't even begin to understand the power of wild animals, which is why they can't appreciate the hazards in working with them. I once had a panther reach under the bars of a cage to grab my arm, and each individual claw was like a steel robot finger drawing me closer to where I would, presumably, be transformed into Annie tartar.

But the average person never seems to get this. In England, panthers used to be for sale at Harrod's for you to take home to your flat. Can you believe that? It may seem funny to imagine some arrogant lawyer in his Bond Street tailoring being trapped for over sixteen hours in his bathroom because his fluffy "kitty" has grown to 75 pounds and suddenly acquired a taste for human flesh (and it is hilarious). But it's also an outrage to sell such incredible, beautiful creatures like toys to nitwits who have no business caring for them.

Kent and I have a reputation as the "go to" people in our area of Florida when it comes to exotics, and you can bet your bottom dollar that things happen just as we are getting ready to leave the clinic to go home on Friday night. Case in point. One evening, just as I was looking forward to a glass of my favorite wine and a relaxing lapse into a state of unconsciousness, we got a call from a desperate gentleman. A few inquiries revealed that not only had this man just had a liver transplant himself (and so was physically debilitated), but had kept a cougar illegally for the past 13 years in his backyard garden. Now the cat was ill with pneumonia and the man was in a panic, convinced it was dying and unable to get anyone to help.

Sigh. This is where my "sucker gene" kicks in. I want to be brassy and harsh like Bette Davis in *All About Eve* and say, "Well, buddy, you'd better buckle up because you and the cougar are going to have a bumpy night." But I can't. I never can. It's not that I give much of a shit about the human beings in these scenarios, but I care deeply about the welfare of the creatures involved—and frankly, can't resist one more opportunity to get close to them. That's when the animal-obsessed little girl in me rears her pigtailed head. Kent, though he puts up a good façade of being flinty-hearted and indifferent, is the same way. The gent lived relatively close, so off we went.

You can never be sure about the setup of these residential exotic situations. There's a big difference between a professional enclosure and someone's backyard, and this place was no exception. The man basically had a very large cage where the mountain lion spent most of its time. When the owner and "his cat" were younger, he told us, he used to take it out for a run on a leash. Now, most people can't control an

80-pound Rottweiler, much less one of these beasts. Their sheer speed and strength are phenomenal, and any adult cougar that decided to tear its leash free of its owner's grasp and attack a toddler would be gone. There would be nothing the owner could do.

So as time went on, the man realized that these runs probably weren't a good idea and they stopped. Thus a gorgeous feline had become a cage shut-in, when even in a zoo he would have had the chance to roam around and play with other cats. See why I get so worked up about this?

This cat was *very territorial* about its cage. It had a separate den up a ramp about eight feet off the ground, like a cave. Now, we're supposed to sedate this adult animal that is situated above us and not at all happy that we're there. The owner is no help, as he can barely stand. So we literally entered the lion's den.

There are various methods you can use in this kind of situation. A pole syringe is one possibility, but that requires having a clear shot at the animal, and that is not going to work while he's in the den. Mister Cougar needs to come out. I'm sure Kent would've loved it if I'd raised my hand like I was back in school and shouted, "I want to be the bait! I want to be the bait! Let me just stand here and you can shoot him as he comes to get me." Let the record show that for a change, I did NOT volunteer to do this.

Another option was to shoot a sedative into his mouth. Sounds risky, I know, but this cat was so sluggish and sick that we were able to get close enough to fire a stream of medication into his mouth, using a combination of drugs. We eventually got him sedated enough so that Kent could examine him and listen to his heart and lungs. The cat was in really bad shape. Sedation is necessary to examine dangerous animals, but it can also be dangerous, and Kent realized that this animal was in critical condition. If he had been a normal kitty, he'd have been in a cage in our offices with a nebulizer and IV fluids.

At that point the dangers of sedation became clear: the cat quit breathing altogether. Quickly we set about our revival efforts. The particular drug we used has a revival agent that you're told works quickly. What the manufacturer doesn't tell you is that on some animals, it works *immediately*. Once we got the cat breathing again—keep in mind we were inches from it at this point—he awoke instantly in his new guise as, "I Feel So Much Better In My Second Life And By The Way Am I Pissed Off Kitty."

At times like this, I'm afraid that my true nature comes out, and it's not flattering. I couldn't have cared less about Kent. As far as I was concerned it was each man for himself as I bolted for the door. I started running with no intention of stopping. But I was brought to a screeching stop by my husband, who had decided that this would be an opportune time to give the cougar fluids! We'd managed to get a noose around the animal's neck while he was out, so at least he was restrained, yet somehow he reminded me of Hannibal Lecter: barely tied down and quite capable of eating my liver with some fava beans.

More sedation was too risky, so we gave the cougar fluids subcutaneously, putting the needle just under the folds of the neck for slow absorption. Now, the average IV line is 72 inches long. I can assure you that when you are near a snarling beast whose sole intention is not so much to live but to kill you to balance out the nature of things, 72 inches is *nothing*. My job was to hold the bag of fluids. Kent had the nearer and more hazardous role of getting the needle in the cougar's neck. Every time Kent got close, the cat snarled at him and I jumped back, pulling the needle out. Kent was getting angry and swearing at me —"God damn! Stand still!"—as though I was jumping away from a snarling predator just to piss him off.

When I am under stress I have these mantras. When I'm on a plane, my mantra goes like this, "I don't want to die. I don't want to die." That day, under those circumstances, it was, "I hate you! I really hate you!" To make a long story short, we got the IV in and the cougar survived. I'm not so sure about the owner.

In times of animal-related stress, "I hate you!" is a reliable go-to phrase. I did embellish it once when Kent sent me down the cow chute after a 2000-pound bull. It was my 120 pounds assigned to stop one ton of snot-spewing bovine flesh with no escape route. Then my mantra became, "I really hate you and I don't want to see your face for the rest of the day!" That's something more for special occasions.

CHAPTER SIX

Hump Daze

Once upon a time, I had a petting zoo that had a camel as one of the attractions. Now that I've owned a camel, I will never own another one. There are several reasons for this antipathy. One is the charming bull camel habit of pissing down his legs to impress the ladies. Camel fur on the inside of the legs is a very wooly coat, and it would be hard to express how eye watering the stench is when that fur has been soaking in urine for weeks. I just don't get the appeal, but apparently to lady camels it's a combination of Viagra and a blue Tiffany box.

The first day we took over an old petting zoo and resort, we sent down a lab tech from our clinic who decided that she, too, would like zoo life. She was the first one to arrive to do the morning shift. That morning she called me and asked, "I thought you said we had a camel. Where's the camel kept?"

I figured she was still waking up. After all, a camel is eight feet tall of grousing, spitting stink. Hard to miss. "Yeah, well it's there," I said. "You can't miss it." But she was right.

Our camel was missing. The zoo was situated along International Drive, sort of the Las Vegas Strip of Orlando, the main drag where all the tourist-related businesses gather in a sort of miles-long blur of consumer delirium. Apparently, someone had left the door open and the camel decided to take go walkabout on International Drive. I guess he wanted to get to Sea World—perhaps to see penguins and other familiar desert animals—because he made a lot of effort in that direction.

Like any good boss, I gave directions over the phone: "Just get down there and bring the camel back!" God bless her, that intrepid lab technician did just that. She's now a vet so it didn't put her off too much.

Another reason I hate camels is that they are as sexually voracious as Tila Tequila but without her restraint and decorum. Camels are very sexual beasts and mature really early. When males hit puberty, their behavior goes from bad to fucking intolerable. One ex-Marine who came to the zoo almost learned the hard way that you aren't supposed to stand directly in front of camels because they will wrap their legs around you and press down to try and break your back. After that close call, we decided we had to castrate the camel. With pleasure.

Believe it or not, this was actually something we had not done. There just hadn't been a need. I'm sure if we lived in Saudi Arabia, we'd have done hundreds by now. Not back then. But there's always a book to read, so we read up on camel castration. Turns out that the way you separate a camel from its cherished junk is much the same as the way you do it to a bull: sedate or distract the animal, strike with the speed of a cobra to sever the testicles, then back the hell away fast. Okay. That part we could handle. What had us confounded was where we were going to do the deed.

The way the facility was set up, we had two choices, neither of them ideal:

- One: Do it at the front of the property, right beside International Drive. I admit, we could've made some money with that. Imagine, you're fresh from the House of Mouse and thinking, "God, if I have to endure one more sticky-sweet piece of children's entertainment, I'm going to develop diabetes." Then you see a camel being forcibly separated from its boys by the side of the road. We could serve hard liquor and call it The Nut Shack. Then again, since most of our patrons were children, that that might not be a good advertisement, especially since we would have to sedate the camel completely.
- Two: We could go to the back of the property, a strip of fenced-in grass right beside Interstate 4, the primary north-south highway through the Orlando metro area. The only difference would be the speed of the passersby and the lack of a standing-room-only crowd.

Sometimes, you're damned if you do and damned if you don't. We chose the option that would give us the maximum chance for embarrassment: number two.

I don't have any idea how many accidents we caused as people got whiplash driving by at 70 mph saying, "Honey, do you want to go to Universal next or—what the HELL is THAT?" Poor Kent had to perform his first camel castration in front of a fast moving audience. It must have seemed like either a very radical ad for cigarettes or the most twisted piece of performance art in Florida history.

There are always risks with anesthesia on big, exotic beasts, so you're grateful if they just come out of it and everything looks good. Everything did look good with the I-4

Camel except for one thing: he developed a horrible scrotal swelling. Sometimes you'll have one that just does that. It looked like he had a couple of watermelons back there.

You've got him on antibiotics, but it's not like you can keep him in a small sterile cage. As a result, you're constantly looking at this monstrous scrotum all day. It just so happened that we went to Kent's university while we were visiting his mom in Missouri. His large animal professor was still there and they castrate lots of llamas. Kent said, "I'm going to see him and find out if he has an answer for this." Kent's professor assured us that scrotal swelling—the camel's, not Kent's—was very common. "Just go and buy 20 boxes of Preparation H and put it on the area," he said. "You'll be amazed what will happen."

This was the one time I pulled rank. There was no way in hell I was going to a pharmacist in the Orlando area and ask for 20 boxes of Preparation H! After the snickering died down, the pharmacy staff would assume Kent and I were into the kinkiest sex games this side of reality television. So I sent some poor unsuspecting technician who, because she worked for us, had no social life to speak of anyway. On went the Preparation H, and damned if things didn't shrink right down. I suspect the technician's social life might actually have perked up as well.

**PART TWO:
FUNNY FARM**

CHAPTER SEVEN

Is That a Squirrel In Your Pants, Or Are You Just Happy to See Me?

I am blessed with that rarest of creatures, the patient husband. Kent has stood by and allowed me to pursue my dreams even when the poor, trusting fool ultimately paid the price of my living them. One such dream had been a standby for years and probably first began fermenting in my fertile little brain when I had read my first books revolving around zoos. In other words, upon reaching adulthood I was the born-every-minute sucker that the exotic animal industry has thrived on for hundreds of years.

The business of buying and selling exotic creatures is full of charlatans and con men who are well aware that when it comes to lions, tigers and bears, we animal lovers have the emotional detachment of a 14-year-old girl at a Justin Bieber concert. The hucksters know we've read our James Herriot and that we're half convinced that the canoe rowing, bowtie wearing denizens of *The Wind in the Willows* really are accurate representations of the mole, toad and badger.

If they weren't peddling home zoos and giraffe preserves, they would be working the phones in boiler rooms and selling kindly little old ladies "shares" in some "can't miss" Ponzi scheme like characters right out of a David Mamet play. In a nutshell, they're slick. They knew exactly how to sell the dream of animal entrepreneurship to the starry-eyed and gullible…in other words, me.

My dream had been to own a petting zoo. I didn't want big cats or elephants; I just wanted to have some everyday farm animals, maybe a llama or two (if nothing else, I could make some comfy sweaters from the wool), and a selection of unusual rodents and insects. My goal was to create my own little world inhabited entirely by creatures that children could hold and touch—to allow those children to be close to creatures just as I had longed for when I was a child.

Well, as luck would have it, there was an animal exhibit that had operated for years in a well-known tourist area in Orlando, and the gent who ran it wanted to concentrate on the helicopter rides that he ran out of the same facility. Smart man. Helicopters may be expensive up front, but they don't require food or shelter, don't bite or run away, and never get friendly with one another on summer nights in the hangar and pop out an unexpected litter of eggbeaters or ceiling fans.

I was delighted. This looked like a fun project and from what we were told would earn us some extra pocket money and very possibly pay for itself. Kent, however, was deeply skeptical. It is very important that I cover for my beloved here. He is a typical midwesterner from Missouri with a "show me" attitude that has been a very useful business asset. Nobody teaches doctors and vets about running a practice in school; they either spend even more time attending business training, or they learn on the job, which can be disastrous when you have six figures worth of student loans hanging around your neck. He did not want to attempt this new venture, but I can be quite a steamroller when I need to be. So I batted my long, lush eyelashes. I pouted fetchingly in the front room of our house. I was even considering going nuclear—withholding sex—when he wisely capitulated and let me have my little petting zoo.

In the end it was probably a wise fiscal calculation; I suspect Kent concluded that paying for the feeding and upkeep of several dozen small furry critters would be cheaper than turning me loose to brand name shop at all the delightful outlets dotted around the Orlando area. And as the saying goes, if that ain't true, it ought to be.

Eau de Camel

And so we found ourselves the proud owners of a petting zoo. I spent a quite delightful few weeks buying up all kinds of critters not known for their propensity to devour small children: goats, sheep, pigs, ferrets, flying squirrels and a veritable cornucopia of kid-friendly beasties. The facility also came complete with what must have been the petting zoo equivalent of heated leather seats and satellite radio: a camel and two llamas, animals that I quickly learned to hate for their bad temper and spitting abilities.

The camel was a real eye opener; I didn't realize that a male camel's idea of "Hey, baby, come and get me" cologne is to piss down his back legs and let it warm up nicely in the sun, producing a stink that could melt cubic zirconium at 20 paces. In addition, I learned never to hold a camel by standing directly in front of it, because one of their less charming habits (which I mentioned earlier) is that they will cross their front legs around yours, arch their necks in an "S" curve and then bear down on your back in an attempt to break it. Suffice it to say that if camels were on the critically endangered list, I would be the one opening a restaurant specializing in camel steaks and organizing my own hunt.

After spending a small fortune cleaning up the facility and buying cages and cash registers, passing all the necessary inspections and dipping into the college funds for liability insurance, we threw the doors open and awaited the flood of eager punters willing to fork over some of their hard-earned for the privilege of allowing our rodents to take up residence in their hair and our goats to eat their children's dungarees.

I think we took in $25 the first day, which just about covered the sheep's feed for a week. Undaunted (or perhaps just deluded; it's so hard to tell the difference), we pressed on. We would open the zoo each day in the late morning and remain open until nine at night. There was a strategy behind this: late in the evening was when the tourists would be red-eyed and exhausted from dragging their screaming, sugar-addicted offspring around the Disney and Universal parks but still needed to give the kids something to burn off the last of their glucose until they passed out in the back seats of the rental minivan. Hence our petting zoo became an unofficial Parents' Paradise, a place where overwhelmed and underslept grownups could leave their rug rats in perfect safety and retreat to the vehicle for a quick yet refreshing coma.

My hubby and I would start our day at 5:30 in the morning, make the 35-mile trip to deliver hay and other supplies to the zoo, work at our clinics until 4:30, and then I would drive down again to run the zoo in the evening. My two kids, who were five and eight at the time, were fantastic. The little entrepreneurs asked me to buy them safari outfits, and so, dressed up like miniature zookeepers, they would lead the ferrets or camel up the road handing out flyers to passersby. My little pimps.

I can only hope that what they missed out on as far as a "normal" life they made up for in learning how to run a business and hustle for your keep. So far, that seems to have been the case, and we enjoy looking at the photographs from those years and telling their friends how they were zookeepers.

Simon the Flying Squirrel
One of the most delightful creatures in our untidy but lovable collection was the tiny baby muntjac deer, Flora. Muntjac deer are the oldest species of deer, going back 15 million years or so. They are also known as "barking deer" since they emit a strange doglike barking sound to alert each other of danger. At maturity the largest ones will still only reach 20 inches at the shoulder, so our Flora was just a slip of a thing and very, very gentle. As we were still bottle-feeding her when we opened, she was a great draw for the kids, who would very quietly sit next to her for the privilege of giving her lunch.

Another favorite was Simon the flying squirrel. He was always happy to come out and be held and he would often shoot down someone's shirt and tickle them until they were giggling helplessly. These energetic bundles of cuteness are actually regarded as pests in this area of the country, as they live in attics and cause untold damage by burrowing into insulation and the like. Not this young squirrel. He excelled in bringing a smile to the sternest of faces. He would glide up to 20 feet from visitor to visitor using the remarkable flap of skin stretched between his extended forepaws and rear legs. It was a beautiful sight.

Apparently, Simon was too popular for his own good. One day he was nowhere to be found. Normally, this gregarious rodent was charming the socks off (and thankfully, the money out of) our guests, but he had apparently vanished. By chance I struck up conversation with a visitor to the zoo. He seemed anxious and I wondered if something had happened on the facility. Then my eye…let me clarify something here and now. I'm a happily married woman. I don't make a habit of openly surveying the lumps in other men's pants. But I couldn't help noticing that there seemed to be a lot of…activity…in this gent's pants. It looked distinctly as though something was squirming around, wildly looking for a path to escape. I suspected that Simon had been squirrel-napped.

It's not often in this life that one has the chance to ask questions that truly have the potential to turn every head in the room. Most of us will never be presented with the opportunity to utter such breathless phrases as, "And then you strangled him with his necktie, didn't you?" or "What was the intern's name, Mr. President?" This was one of those moments, maybe the only one I would ever have. I seized it.

Calmly and with all the irony I could muster, I said, "Pardon me, but do you have my squirrel in your pants?" Looking back I could have got an entirely unwelcome reply, but actually the real one wasn't much better. The man got a look on his face like a 16-year-old caught sneaking in at 3 a.m. "A squirrel?" he said.

The innocent act wasn't going to work with me. I was going to crack him like an egg. "Yes," I said. "Why is he there?"

"Because he seems to like it in there."

I had no reply to that. The man blushed and fished Simon out of his pants, and we put our prize flyer back in his large housing area, from then on padlocking the door and only allowing closely supervised handlings. I was just grateful that Simon hadn't panicked at being trapped in the guy's boxer shorts. The publicity generated by the headline, "Man receives vasectomy from live squirrel," probably wouldn't have done much for business.

The Final Straw

Aside from the monetary losses and constant exhaustion from running back and forth between work places, the petting zoo experience was everything I could have hoped it would be. Really. Okay, I'm lying. As most childhood dreams do when they grow into adult reality, the result looks more like Kansas and less like Oz. We had insurance companies and lawyers and inspectors, oh my. So when an event took place that sealed the fate of my petting zoo dream, it wasn't entirely unwelcome.

One of our favorite functions at the zoo was the birthday party. Groups of up to 15 kids would spend a few hours with the animals learning about their backgrounds and generally playing zookeeper, with feeding time being the highlight of the day. This would take place after hours to allow the party guests special one-on-one time with the animals. So imagine my surprise one night when the facility was closed for a party and I was midway through explaining the feeding habits of a 17-foot python when I noticed large groups of strangers walking around the facility, petting the animals.

When you own a facility that hosts the public, you are very focused on your insurance liability, and at this moment I knew I did not have enough staff coverage to ensure safety for more than the group we already were servicing. I excused myself, turned and in the dark, bumped into our zoo manager, who had returned from his day off.

I'm not going to bore you with the details of our conversation, but suffice to say, the manager was waiting for our business to close for the day, bringing in exotic animals such as cougars, bringing in his own clients for a late-night visit to the big cats and such, charging them using my register, closing everything down and taking the money. I was none the wiser.

I was shocked at the betrayal, and also at his stupidity and brazenness. It wasn't hard for me to imagine the consequences if a member of the public had been injured by a big cat on my property when we did not have insurance to cover such injuries because we weren't supposed to *have* such animals! I'll spare you the ugliness other than to say that at that moment, the Irish in me came to the forefront. I let my husband know he was right and we moved all our animals out in the space of two hours. To this day, I remain convinced that it's really the humans, not the squirrels, snakes and goats, who belong in the cages.

Except for the camels. I still hate those fuckers.

CHAPTER EIGHT

Deer Diary

When your petting zoo goes belly-up, what do you do with 57 animals? Well, if you have a farm, some of them they continue to live in happy retirement, playing bocce ball, bitching about the food, complaining that the kids never call and all the other things retirees do. But what about the critters that don't belong on a farm? You thank God for anybody willing to transport various un-housebroken animals in the back seats of their cars. We found homes for all the animals, including Flora the muntjac deer, who now lives on a luxury estate with several other muntjac friends. However, her departure was not without drama...naturally.

While I searched for a suitable home for her, Flora lived with us at home in the back yard of our golf-front home, which was in an exclusive neighborhood. At night she would sleep in her crate and all was well for a time. But no matter how careful you are, accidents happen. One day someone who shall remain nameless failed to properly secure the gate on her crate, and she made her escape onto the fourth tee of the golf course.

This was a nightmare. First, there was the obvious difficulty in running down a deer, which cheetahs have a hard enough time doing, much less little old me. But my main concern was that Flora would run the short distance to the main road and be killed, or disappear into the adjacent state park and be lost forever—and in all likelihood become some predator's dinner. I decided I would have to try to lure her close to me and somehow slip a leash on her.

Seemed a good plan (these things always seem like a good plan before I actually try to execute them), but I did not account for the giddy sense of freedom that had infected Flora. She had gone from a docile petting zoo deer to a scared, skittish beast on the run. It was a very hot, humid summer day in Florida, about 97 degrees at two in the afternoon; not ideal deer-catching weather. But I walked out onto the golf course with treats in my hand...and it quickly became apparent that Flora was not interested in the food. The chase was on!

Fortunately, this stupid deer did nothing more than run around and around our house. By continually chasing after her I was at least keeping her from veering back onto the golf course and surprising some poor duffer into a heart attack in the middle of his backswing. The minutes went by, I became hotter and sweatier, and my language got fouler and fouler. It may not jibe with your impression of the sylphlike English rose that I am, but my language regularly makes sailors blush. Adding to my frustration, the crowd watching this spectacle grew bigger and bigger. I think at some point ESPN may have been called.

After about a half hour, I was completely exhausted and starting to feel dangerously overheated. I knew that in this heat I couldn't go much longer without ending up with heatstroke. In desperation, I waited for Flora to round the corner of the house, and then I flew through the air at her in a most impressive imitation of an NFL cornerback taking out a wide receiver. No flags were thrown. Seriously, I must have been three feet off the ground and in full flight when I brought her down. So I can definitively answer one age-old question: it IS possible to catch a deer with your bare hands! I would have been the toast of any hunter-gatherer tribe waiting for its dinner.

The deer screamed like a woman and her razor-like hoof entered my mouth and slit the roof as efficiently as a chef's knife. I felt blood pour onto my tongue, but I didn't care! I had taken down my prey as efficiently and ruthlessly as any African lioness picking off an impala from the herd. I felt calm and competent.

"Get the fucking crate!" I screamed to my children, oblivious to the applause that had erupted from the spectators. The kids ran up with the crate, I pushed Flora in, slammed the door shut and tried to beat a graceful retreat into the house before I collapsed. My children, accustomed to my desperate and often ridiculous actions around animals, were not as impressed.

"Mom," said my youngest, "Did you know you said the "S" word seven times and the "F" word twelve?"

"I don't care," I snarled.

"Oh, I was just letting you know because my principal is over there."

CHAPTER NINE

The Special Needs Chicken

Every so often I get to play mommy to animals that are less threatening than Sammy the testosterone-poisoned chimp. At such times, I get to relive the days when my girls were little, but without the potential for tantrums and dirty diapers. One of those occasions involved Susannah, the special needs chicken.

Susannah was just another chicken until she earned the enmity of a rough-tough rooster we had just acquired. This was one mean cock, supposedly bred for fighting in Mexico. One day, Susannah crossed him and he clocked her on the head with his beak, sending her into an instant coma. She had tremendous brain swelling (which may seem impossible because a chicken's brain isn't that big to begin with) and I spent three weeks looking after her, feeding her and giving her medication. Plus her temperature regulator must've gone out because her comb was so hot—she was like a roast chicken.

After three weeks she came out of this coma, but she thought down was up and up was down. So she would put her head between her legs, thinking she was standing straight, try to walk and instantly fall over. It would have been hysterical if—no, it was hysterical. But I decided I would make our special needs chicken into my pet project, pardon the pun.

I made Susannah a neck brace out of a hair scrunchy, like a car accident victim with whiplash. She couldn't walk very well, so I taught her how to walk again. How does one teach a chicken to walk? That sounds like the setup for a joke, but I'm quite serious. I would literally place her feet one in front of the other; I did it every day for seven months.

Finally, she was ready to solo. I called everyone outside to see my handiwork, the test drive of my special student. I felt like a proud parent at the school play. My protégé took three steps, then fell into a somersault and rolled down the hill, which, when you really stop and think about it, is quite impressive in itself. Everyone said, "Is that it?" but I was delighted.

The reality is that animals don't live as long as we do. But what I've learned is that every animal has something to teach us. First of all, they have no apparent perception of or fear of death. They also don't worry about how things are supposed to be; they deal with the now and the way things are. To watch a chicken over a span of seven months learning to walk again is really something. Their average lifespan might be 10 years, so seven months is equal to about 10 years in our time. Would you have the patience to do 10 years of physical therapy just to walk a few steps? I wouldn't.

A month later, Susannah was pretty much back to normal—walking around the yard, feeding herself, sleeping with our dogs in the dog run. I was so proud; rehab on a chicken is not easy. Then our local fox ate her and left only a pile of feathers. I'm sure there's a lesson in there somewhere, but I'll be damned if I know what it is.

CHAPTER TEN

All Things Sweaty And Stinky

I had wanted to be a farmer's wife since age three. Don't ask me why, but when the other little girls in my neighborhood in England were trying on sparkly princess dresses, I was modelling little bib overalls for my perplexed parents. When I met Kent, who is a year older than I am, I asked him, "What did you want to be when you were four years old?" He replied, "A farmer." Now, he may have just been saying that to get me into the sack (for the record, it worked), but the inescapable conclusion was that we were perfect for each other.

When I was five or six years old, I read a book called *Willow Farm* by Enid Blyton, a wonderful, very old-fashioned English writer from the 1920s who wrote children's mysteries like the "Famous Five." I absolutely loved these books, and after reading *Willow Farm* I wanted to have pigs and chickens and donkeys, because everything in this book was idyllic. So in my mind, that was what my farm would be like. Now, my childhood was rather un-countrified, while Kent was in Missouri with his father in the country delivering piglets and things like that. But when we had been together for about a year, it became inevitable that we would own our own farm. We went for a drive one day north of Orlando, saw the piece of land where we live now, and—you should pardon the expression—bought the farm. So there we were, the childhood farmer and the childhood farmer's frau, about to make our bucolic dream come true.

And other than the pee, poop, sex, death, violence and constant work, it was everything we thought it could be.

Bovine Intervention

But before we even built our house, we decided we needed cows. Don't ask me why. We just felt that if we were going to be farmers, we were going to need cows. Kent wasn't practicing as a large animal veterinarian per se, but he'd grown up pulling calves and doing other very manly farm things, so I figured he could help me through the rough spot. Never mind that in the beginning, he *was* the rough spot.

Getting our first six cows involved a four-hour drive on a chilly Florida day. Normally, when you buy cattle, the sellers have already put them in a pen, but when we pulled up, the scene was an open hundred-acre field with the cows just tiny spots milling around way at the other end. Somehow, we were supposed to choose our six beasts from among about two hundred cows with no one to help us. The rancher was recovering from leg surgery and was of no use to us. So Kent looks at me and, like he's talking to a border collie, says, "Go and bring the cows down."

This went over very well. I'm a deeply submissive woman and I enjoy being ordered about as if I'm a character from the movie *Babe*. But I actually started to obey. I found myself running along this huge field toward this herd of cattle, sweating and shedding layers of clothing, while Kent and the rancher chatted away. Finally I came to my senses, stopped, said, "Fuck this," turned to my beloved and shouted, "You get them!"

Unfortunately, the cows didn't care for my tone or something, and before I knew it they were out of the field and running down the road toward disaster. I could smell cowshit and lawsuit on the air. Then someone from the ranch opened a gate and got the cows into a yard. Kent waded in among them and chose the half dozen animals we would take home, using the highly discerning method of picking whichever ones were confused enough to walk into our trailer.

The next three hours were spent towing four tons of reluctant bovine along the highway behind our little Toyota. We were trying not to jackknife and enduring endless horn bleats from drivers. They saw that one of the cows had lay down in the trailer and assumed that the other 600 people who'd already passed us had failed to make us aware of the situation. I fumed at Kent and just wanted to get home. Thus began my career as the world's first two-legged herding dog.

Foreplay on the Farm

Let's test your farmhouse math, shall we? We have cows. We want calves. So we need..? Very good. We need a bull. Or more to the point, bull semen. In an effort to put our ladies in a family way without enduring the tantrums of a 1500-pound ruminant of the male persuasion, we had tried artificial insemination. This is not the picnic that you might imagine. Basically, it involves vials of bull semen, very, very long gloves, and putting most of your lower arm in a place that probably would have left the late Steve Irwin, the great Crocodile Hunter, shaking his head and saying, "Uh-uh. You first." Shockingly, we tired of this activity—and our cows weren't getting pregnant—so we decided that we needed to bite the bullet and get us a bull.

Now, imagine for a second that you're a young bull. You weigh three-quarters of a ton with horns that can rip a man open. You're the badass of the barnyard, king of all you survey. Now you hear that you're going to be tested to see if you're fertile. Cool, you think, as the rancher and a vet lead you into a narrow chute. This is going to be fun. I'm going to prove my incredible bull machismo. And then the vet sticks an electric cattle prod up your ass and turns it on, making you immediately ejaculate with no foreplay whatsoever. Not even a dirty magazine to get you in the mood. This is how bulls are tested for fertility. You can imagine what this does to their disposition.

Now you have a picture of what must be one of the most insane transactions on the planet. While you're driving out to pick up your nice, docile bull, the rancher does something to it that wasn't done to the prisoners at Abu Ghraib, transforming it into 1,500 pounds of panicked, pissed-off Mack truck hell-bent on destruction. Then he says, "OK, he's all yours, take him away!" This animal didn't want to go anywhere, but somehow we got him into our trailer, which he dwarfed, and spent the next hour thinking he was going to rip it apart and force us off the road.

The drive must have caused temporary brain damage, because when we got the bull to the farm (he was beginning to calm down after smelling female cows), we had the bright idea to put him in our chute, where we could vaccinate him, deworm him and get him ready to go. What we failed to take into account was the fact that the last time this bull had been in a chute, only two hours before, he had been violated in a most unseemly high-voltage manner. Mr. Bull went into the chute, realized where he was, and proceeded to *climb the seven-foot walls* of this enclosure try to escape.

Well, all I can say is that you haven't lived until you've seen a three-quarter-ton bull with its torso draped over the top of a wall, balancing and unable to move. Finally, he did a half-assed somersault off the wall and we let him out of the chute. Nobody got any shots that day except for me and Kent. Ours were tequila.

CHAPTER ELEVEN

Days of Swine and Roses

I like to tell people that we're basically George Orwell's *Animal Farm*, but with a more sinister undertone. We're sure as hell not *Charlotte's Web*, though I am a great saver of spiders, which I consider to be vital parts of the farm ecosystem. But it would have been tough to convince someone that we weren't sprung from that E.B. White book when Mr. Piggy, Prince of Pigs (yes, that's his name), entered our lives.

    I didn't want pigs on our farm. I once thought they were the cutest things going, but we had one in the clinic and I discovered that this was in fact not the case. Imagine my surprise one day when I came into the clinic and the girls said to me, "Your pig is here." I replied, "No, it isn't. We're not going to have a pig." They told me someone had brought it in, a little runt that weighed maybe four ounces. You can't imagine how tiny this animal was. He was black spotted, but on his side was a perfect heart shaped marking. My God, I thought. This is Wilbur. So we raised a pig.

When he got to two or three pounds, the time came for the Prince of Pigs to be outside, but because he was smaller than the chickens, they would knock him over and bully him. He spent a long time being scared of chickens, but eventually realized that they were his friends. They would sleep together in the yard, though on occasion a chicken would end up flattened in the morning, a victim of the pig's increasing bulk.

All along I figured that the pig started off weighing about four ounces, so how big could he get? Next silly question. He hasn't had a recent weigh in at Weight Watchers, but I'm guessing that today Mr. Piggy, Prince of Pigs, is 250-300 pounds of pure fat. I think Kent saw him (and may still see him) as mobile bacon, but he's really the sweetest, most amazing animal. He still had a healthy respect for the chickens even at 250 pounds. At night the chickens would sleep by him and even on him. He was no threat; he was too much of a scaredy-pig. Also, pigs are not the neatest of eaters, which meant that the chickens often had their pick of the refuse that the pig left in the wake of his feasting.

Fear of Open Spaces
The truly unusual thing about Mr. Piggy is that he suffers from agoraphobia. He has panic attacks. I know how it sounds, but it's true. He doesn't like to leave his pen to forage in the open, even though I encourage him. But sometimes he breaks free with these great piggy thoughts of acorns and how fun it would be to snuffle under the trees and then he realizes, "Oh, where am I?"

Instead of retracing his steps (which he could do; pigs have an amazing sense of smell), he lets out panicky grunts for help until I come. I'll head out to the field and tell him, "It's alright Mr. Piggy, I'm here." He has these sharp tusks and six inches of hair, and he looks frightening because the hair stands up. But he is just a frightened piggy and the gentlest thing on four legs. I can tickle him behind the ears and all 250 pounds flop to the ground! He likes me to tickle the bottom of his feet. Then I pull out his bottom lip and check his teeth.

The simple fact is that he could bite my hand off in a second if he wanted to. But he never, ever would. You have to know him. I can sit on him and we can have a piggy bonding moment. Now he's ten years old, and this particular breed suffers from arthritis. So every now and again we try to put him on a diet. It's the only time he gets angry. In general, this is a pig with some self-esteem issues and a sensitive ego. Right now he's bonded to a sheep, and I think it's because it's the only animal he's ever been able to boss around. He pretends to bite the sheep and gets a mouth full of wool. The sheep doesn't give a shit, but it's very important for Mr. Piggy's dignity and sense of self.

The Pig of the Month Club
The other trauma for Mr. Piggy was that he found the appearance of other pigs on the farm very stressful. I don't think he's ever realized that he's a pig. He thinks he's a human who just needs a shave and some serious dental work. Now, my younger daughter, Becky, had a passion for pigs, and at ten she came into the kitchen carrying a ten-pound black piglet. She said, "I was just thinking about having a piglet and one appeared in the driveway." Things like that happen around here all the time. Where did this pig come from? Was he gift from God? From Satan? Did someone sign us up for the Pig of the Month Club?

I put this little piggy in a dog crate and immediately he transformed into Damian. Question answered; this was a pig from Hell. He was a pig possessed! Somehow he got through the metal door, and Becky went after him and caught him again. Then suddenly I realized, with a cold shiver down my spine, that this was a wild boar piglet, which would grow into one of the most dangerous animals in the state. This was a potential killer. This was most assuredly *not* Wilbur.

We decided that if we were to let Becky keep her pig, we had to neuter him. So a few weeks later, Kent injected him with a sedative. We waited. And waited. Finally, Hell Pig took off like a bat out of…well, you know. We followed, but this time Becky couldn't catch him. The sedative was having no effect, and looking back it should have been obvious that it wouldn't. Pigs are impervious to rattlesnake venom. It gets absorbed in their fat. They will actually dig out and eat rattlesnakes, which makes them the best organic rattlesnake clearance tool around, though probably not ideal for residential use since you'll also end up with great furrows six feet long in your yard.

So here's this pig that's had a big dose of sedative for its size and he's bolting for the woods at about 25 mph with us running after. It must've been very amusing for the other animals on the farm to watch the spectacle. Then—boom! All of a sudden, Hell Pig fell on his side, panting, as the drugs finally took effect. We stopped, and then fell to our knees, panting, as the run and the fact that we're out of shape took effect. But just as we were trying to figure out how to haul this swine (which now weighed 35 pounds) back to the house, he came alive again. Off we went on the merry chase, Damian the Hell Pig followed by the People Who Wanted to Cut His Balls Off.

In the end, we realized that there was no pen that was going to hold this beast. He was mean as hell and frankly dangerous even at 35 pounds, and he was going to get a lot bigger. So we kept him in a trailer that you could hose out without actually going in.

Why didn't we get rid of him? Because we're hopelessly stubborn and stupid. But you should be glad. If not for my and Kent's stubbornness, this book wouldn't be half as funny.

Makin' Bacon

Other than Mr. Piggy, we refused for years to have pigs because of the astounding amount of pig poop that they produce. They also eat an astonishing amount of food, which of course has a direct relationship to the poop. Did you see the *Simpsons Movie*, where Homer talked about his pet pig filling a silo with his shit in three days? I have it on good authority that that's an understatement.

For a while, we had three breeding pigs: a Yorkshire boar who when he stood up on his hind feet had an almost rabid look (he would froth at the mouth), weighed 800-900 pounds and was seven-and-a-half feet tall. This thing was pure feral fury, and we never named him. We braved keeping him around only for the savagery of his sperm. But he demanded caution. If you were not upright and able to move fast when you came near him, you would be eaten.

We also had two females—Mary and Lola—who weighed 600-700 pounds. Lola was just gorgeous. And we had ten-year-old human female Becky, who had quite an affinity for pigs. She and I would care for these animals together. We had an automated feeding and watering system, but no system for cleaning them. We had to do that by hand twice a day, which took an hour and a half each time—three hours a day of piggy poo.

Eventually the females had babies—14 of them. And even though pigs are good parents, some of the babies are inevitably squished by their mothers, who weigh about a thousand times more than they do. That's a hard lesson for a little girl to learn. Well, in one of the litters, we had a runt, and Kent referred to it as a "knock it on the head," because on a working farm where the livestock was the livelihood, the farmer would often knock such a runt on the head and kill it rather than invest the time in nursing a pig that wouldn't likely survive. But Becky didn't get the terminology, and she named the runt "Knock It On the Head Sam."

Knock It On the Head Sam was with us for about four days before he succumbed to his smallness, despite all the work we did to save him. However, he inspired Becky to write the most amazing story. She was truly a pig prodigy.

She would go out to these beasts, short little thing that she was, just hop on their backs and ride. This made her a rock star in the eyes of some of her classmates, who wouldn't dream of doing something so crazy! Sometimes she would fall off and she would just laugh. She was happy, dare I say, as a pig in shit. I think perhaps she was a pig in another life.

However, the time came when I decided that three hours of shoveling pig crap wasn't worth the trouble. The clincher was when I was recovering from a serious surgery and I was on Demerol, the only thing that would kill the indescribable pain I was in. One day, I realized that my pack of 13 young pigs, which were the size of small dogs (10-30 pounds), all needed their daily feeding and checking for injuries and pests. Now, you may ask me, "Annie, why on earth didn't you wait for your husband or kids to get home and do that for you, you silly shit?" All I can say, your honor, is that it didn't occur to me at the time.

When I got into the pen, the young pigs all came rushing at me to be fed. I was dizzy from the medication, but I could see that the situation was quickly becoming dangerous. All of a sudden, one of the pigs grabbed my calf muscle and bit. I realized that unless I got free, I might lose the use of the entire muscle—and that might be the least of my worries. I pulled away; fortunately my jeans were loose and the entire pant leg ripped off in the pig's mouth. Now, I was down in the corner of the pigpen high as a kite on Demerol, with my only weapon being my feet. Did I mention that I was wearing flip-flops? Not the best footwear for fending off a pack of provocative porcine persecutors. The flip-flops disappeared into the muck and pig poop.

Picture it if you can: me like Ralph Macchio in *The Karate Kid*, doing a drug-induced series of kung fu kicks toward a baker's dozen of hungry pigs, fighting to escape with my life and not become piggy dinner. I slowly advanced (I suspect the pigs were simply too doubled over with piggy hilarity to really attack me with any vigor) and got out of the pen in one piece.

Once outside, with the door slammed shut, I decided on the spot that a freezer full of bacon was more appealing than shoveling pig poop. I can say with satisfaction that the next year yielded the most satisfying sausage, pork chops and ham I have ever tasted in my life.

CHAPTER TWELVE

Horses, Goats and Sheep...Oh My!

At the time that Mr. Piggy was coming of age, we also had a 42 year-old horse named Casey. As far as we knew, this was the oldest horse on the planet. Casey had been with us from the beginning. She had taught hundreds of kids to ride, come into the house when we were building it and eaten chunks of drywall, and christened what would become our lounge with her feces. Kent had a theory that the horse actually died 15 years earlier, but he electrical signals twitched the odd muscle here and there and created the illusion of life.

Casey was a steady horse who did nothing really unexpected. Every now and then, she would throw a fit just to see if it would work, essentially telling us, "No, I'd rather not go out today and work, I'd rather stay here and eat." And she ate *everything*. Once Casey, the dog and a duck were all fighting over the dog bowl, snapping at each other. This was when I had first come to America and while we had a nice bit of land, we lived in a trailer with steep metal steps.

That damned horse actually walked up the steps one day and into the trailer in the hopes that there was food somewhere! She was a total food slut. She would break into the feed bins to get her fix. I wondered how long it would be before she was like a meth addict, shoplifting from the local convenience store to service her alfalfa habit.

Now, of course, the trouble with eating everything in sight is that you…eat everything in sight. Sometimes, you send your digestive tract objects that make it recoil in horror and go on vacation. With Casey, we got to the point that we said, "This horse is going to eat herself to death." She had a near-miss once when she swallowed a whole corncob that Kent had to then fish out. But did that stop Casey the eating machine? Hell no. She had the gut of a longshoreman.

She was also a great riding horse. My eldest daughter, Christina, was five at the time, but she'd started riding horses at three years old. I have no idea how she worked out getting on Casey, who wasn't a thoroughbred but was still about 56 inches high (a tidy jump for a kindergartener), but I would look out into the pasture and see Casey galloping off into the distance. I would look closer and think, "What is that speck on her back?" After a minute (mummy is a bit slow on the uptake sometimes) I would realize with horror that yonder speck was my daughter standing in the stirrups pretending to be some Hungarian Cossack in the circus.

I thought, "Oh God!" She did this wide sweep of the pasture at full gallop, but Casey had such a steady stride that Christina was standing and waving to me like she was riding a plastic horse on the merry-go-round. She has always been an amazing horsewoman.

Casey kept on living and living, and as she got older it became harder and harder to keep weight on her, because horses grind their teeth down to nothing. So we were spending vast amounts of money to find a diet for a horse that couldn't even eat hay. Plus, it was a losing battle because her organs were shutting down. In the meantime, she bonded with Mr. Piggy. She became part of this symbiotic little barnyard trio.

Susannah, the aforementioned Special Needs Chicken, would ride on the back of Mr. Piggy, Prince of Pigs. He in turn would stand contentedly between Casey's legs. Casey would drop grain from her mouth as she ate; this would land on the pig's back and both swine and fowl would have a feast. It was endearing to watch, and over the years the horse and swine became bosom companions. I think Mr. Piggy figured his food was just manna falling from Heaven.

But one learns about life and death in stark terms on the farm. We think that one day Casey had a stroke and went blind. It wouldn't have been a problem if she had stayed in a familiar pasture where she knew where everything was. But the first day, she panicked and fell over on her side. That's when we knew it was time. We had to put our remarkable horse down.

Mr. Piggy, Prince of Pigs, spiralled into a long mourning period. He didn't eat for a week. We would see him, now a large, full-grown pig, standing in the yard where Casey's head collar was, just breathing in her scent. It was terribly sad. I had a friend who had a horse that was allergic to grass (I am not making this up), and needed a place to board this horse, so we brought the horse around and for the first time since Casey's death, Mr. Piggy perked up. He took his place beneath his new horse...and got a wicked bite for his trouble and ran off squealing. I watched and I could see his little piggy brain saying, "Well, that must have been a mistake." So he trotted back over to the new horse and tried again. It wasn't a mistake. Another bite. This sure as hell wasn't Casey.

Sheep Tricks

Today, Mr. Piggy, Prince of Pigs, lives with two sheep. One of them, Pepper, we bought at a 4H event. For those of you who grew up not more than five minutes from an emergency supply of latte and sushi, 4H is a national student farming organization where kids raise animals then sell them at auction to raise money. We went to this 4H event and bid on this sheep, Pepper, and got him. What we didn't know (though I have no idea to this day why everyone *else* seemed to know this) was that you had to take the animal home the same day. That explained all the trailers in the parking lot. We hadn't come with a trailer; we had come in my Mitsubishi Galant with its nice cloth seats.

So into the Galant's back seat went all 120 pounds of Pepper, and we drove home. Along the way, on one of the major thoroughfares through this part of Florida, drivers killed their necks doing double takes. After all, I was sitting in the back seat with a frightened sheep that was screaming constantly.

Then Pepper upped the ante: he adopted a stance that made me certain he was going to urinate. Now, sheep have bladders that can only be called epic; once they start peeing, they can produce a steady stream for at least five minutes. Thank God I had two large towels with me, and as the stream began I used them to catch and deflect all the urine from my cloth seats. No mother bear has ever defended her cubs so diligently. I caught pee with my hands, my clothes, you name it.

But when the stream stopped, not a drop had hit the seats. My Galant was as virginal as when we left the fairground. Lucky thing for Pepper. He's still with us, but if he had ruined my car interior...let's just say I love mutton.

We had another sheep, which I'll call Sarge, who made a habit of rounding up our cows with the precision of a drill sergeant. It was amazing to see. This incredible sheep would decide that the cows had to line up and would force them to stand at parade rest in perfect army formation, like a drill instructor lining up cadets on a parade ground. It was astonishing to watch.

Picture this 140-pound sheep facing down maybe a dozen cows that weigh a half-ton apiece. Even more astonishing, the sheep would whip the 1,500-pound bull into shape as well! And if either cows or bull didn't move fast enough for Sarge the sheep, he would leap in the air and butt the cow right on the ass. The cows would line up, perfectly spaced and all facing the same way, and the sheep would walk up and down in front of them, looking for all the world like a modern major general reviewing his troops. We would howl with laughter from the house and wish we could catch the spectacle on videotape, which we never did.

Eventually, Sarge would wander off to eat some grass or something, but the cows, clearly intimidated, would not budge. They would stay at attention until some silent signal passed between them and the sheep, and then they were dismissed. This went on several times a week and it made the sheep a perfect guardian for the cows and their calves. Sadly, Sarge was killed and eaten by a leopard that escaped from a sanctuary that used to be near our property, which just goes to show you that you shouldn't try to rise above your station.

Goat Pornography
I don't like goats, just to get that out of the way. They have a peculiar odor, and they're pugnacious and eat everything in sight. But when our tourist petting zoo shut down, we ended up keeping some of the goats on our farm and finding homes for the others. We had a Nigerian dwarf goat that we called Satan, because he looked positively diabolical. You know the images of the Devil that appear on classic pentagrams? That was our eerie little goat. We also had Edelweiss and Kahlua, the female goats, and another taller male goat whose name I can't recall. So goats joined our family.

Perhaps it's time to mention the other thing I don't like about goats: they are perverted little bastards. A bit of perversion is laudable in a human being, but I don't really care for it in my farm fauna. A few months after the goats joined our menagerie, we noticed that Kahlua and Edelweiss kept getting their heads stuck in the stock fence. It was really tough to get them out with their horns, so we de-horned them. But Edelweiss would continue to get her head caught. What a stupid animal! Or so we thought.

One day, as we were getting ready to free her from the fence again, we noticed that the two male goats were taking turns gang-banging Edelweiss, non-stop, one after the other. The poor goat was having the daylights shagged out of her! Thinking we were rescuing her from a terrible ordeal, we freed her from the fence...and in about ten seconds she ran back and put her head back in the fence again. The goat rape continued apace. I was shocked. Little Edelweiss was a tramp!

These episodes would go on all afternoon. Neighbors would call us, "I think your goat has her head stuck in the fence." We'd just nod and say, "We know."

All this just reinforced my opinion about goats: not only were they smelly and obnoxious, they were morally bankrupt as well. One other incident cemented this opinion for me. My children were quite fond of bringing their little friends over to see our animals, and for some reason they always ran off to see the goats first. When they came back, they were invariably giggling and shushing each other. After a while my steel-trap parenting instincts told me something was amiss, so I walked quietly down to the goat enclosure to see what was the big deal.

How do I put this? I had never actually seen a goat give himself oral sex, but I have now. It's really very interesting. They put their head between their legs and lick away, curl their lip right up over their nose, and continue this way until they bring themselves to orgasm. And when a goat climaxes, let's just say they're as impressive as the sheep with peeing; they go on forever. No wonder Edelweiss was so happy. If human males could do it, I feel confident that most of them would probably never leave the house. It would change the world.

Imagine the educational value for the children. We even had a male sheep that mated with a female goat and produced a *geep*, which is actually what you call the offspring of that union. They're extremely odd looking and very rare. But in general, the goats were just pains in the ass, screwing everything in sight and constantly getting out of their pen. But eventually, coyotes came in one night and killed them all, which was a convenient solution to the problem, really.

Now when anybody tries to bring us goats, the goats take one look at me and the deal's off. They pass the word down the goat grapevine: *Don't fuck with Annie. She'll call the coyotes. You should see what she did to the cow-herding sheep.*

CHAPTER THIRTEEN

Boyfriend Abuse

Kent and I are really quite devious about spreading around the astonishing amount of work that comes with running an operating farm. First there was the way we would tell friends that we were having a "fencing party" out at the farm and invite them to join us. No doubt they assumed they would be sipping chardonnay while watching strapping young men have at each other with foil and épée, but when they arrived we would hand them a shovel and point them toward a distant spot in the fields, saying, "That's where the post hole needs to be dug." For some reason, we rarely had return guests.

But that's not the only way we took advantage of people's naïve delusions about the pastoral charms of farm life. To this day we breed calves on our 40-acre spread north of Orlando, and every year comes the annual roundup where the young cows are given their shots and so on. Young bulls are de-horned so they won't be a danger, and since we don't want rampant breeding going on, we also perform a brief but dramatic surgery that separates the bulls from some of the most cherished parts of their anatomy. This usually requires a few extra sets of hands, so once upon a time we asked our two teenage daughters' boyfriends to help out. Poor bastards.

One of them had spent at least some time around cows, so he could handle himself. The other one didn't have a clue and showed up in shorts and flip-flops—and then stood rooted to the spot by the spectacle. Once upon a time, vets used all kinds of anaesthetic for castration because they felt sorry for the bull. That caused infections, so now Kent does his thing the old-fashioned way: pulling the bull's tail over its back so it hurts so bloody much the animal doesn't notice the sudden severance of its gonads. I could swear I saw the faces of both these boys—delightful young men who were honestly too nice to be put through the ordeal—pale a few shades as the bull balls hit the ground with a wet thud.

Of course, after the procedure comes the *coup de gras*: Rocky Mountain oysters. Within twenty minutes of being "picked," they were in the frying pan and we had persuaded poor Quentin and Josh to try some. Sitting at the kitchen table, poking with their forks at that soft, squishy mass, they tried not to vomit and, I'm proud to say, succeeded. They even ate a little, the brave guys. It's hard to consume food when all you can think is, "Dude, I feel your pain."

"Don't Lick Your Lips!"
Something about cattle seems to provoke the inadvertent abuse of trusting boyfriends. I think it's because everyone thinks of cows as being so docile and mild-mannered—and because their only exposure to a calf's birth is the scene from *City Slickers*. Needless to say, my daughters' boyfriends had no idea what they were in for when they also got involved in calving season.

Giving birth to a calf sounds simple but it's actually an ordeal involving lots of pulling and terrific effort. Our first calving (before said boyfriends entered the picture), we had a cow who was trying to push her baby out while the bull was trying to push the calf back in! Apparently the bull had decided the calf would become a rival for female affections, so in the grand tradition of aggressive men everywhere, he was sticking it to his rival before said rival had even come into this world.

Well, that didn't sit well with Momma Cow, so she took off, her lover in hot pursuit. Kent and I looked at each other and a thought passed between us in an instant:

"Do we have to do what I think we have to do?"

"Yes, we do."

So off we ran as well. Soon we were all galloping around the fields like the Keystone Kops: the cow trying to give birth, followed by the bull as a sort of self-appointed "reverse obstetrician," followed by me, Kent and several teenagers, screaming at the tops of our lungs, not having the slightest idea what we would do if we caught up to several tons of hysterical cow flesh. Just another day on the farm.

To make a long story short, we managed to distract the bull with some feed long enough for Kent and his helpers to pull the calf out of dear old mom. The bull seemed to lose interest at this point; I suppose once the birth was in the books, he said to hell with it. The calf was fine, though I don't think he and Pa ever shared many "Field of Dreams" father-son moments.

One year our favorite cow, Crystal, who always "threw" a really good calf, had not been herself. Actually, that's a rather egregious piece of British understatement. We thought she had died, because she was lying in a field with her legs straight up in the air. I went so far as to ask our neighbor to shoot her, but when we turned her over we must have moved the calf off a nerve or something because she immediately got up and ran off. Our Viking-esque neighbor put his shotgun, plus the only three shells he owned, away for another day. He didn't seem disappointed. With us, he always knew there would be something to shoot.

So a short while later it came time for Crystal to give birth. This happened to be one of the few times in my life that I was ever sick, and I was sick as a dog. Worse, I was taking my mother to the airport to fly back to England. I only saw her once a year and she had a heart condition, so goodbyes were a wretched, emotional scene. It was late November, dark and cold, and I was feeling miserable and hungry. I came home and Crystal was not looking good. Kent decided we needed to "pull" the calf.

Understand that Billy Crystal could not have done this even if Jack Palance had held a gun to his head while doing one-armed push-ups. Pulling a calf takes titanic effort. It was pitch dark and we got out the calving chains, thick chains that look like something you would use to tie up a boat trailer. Kent and Quentin attached the chains to the calf, we got an IV going into the cow, and we were trying to do all this by flashlight. Then we started pulling, only to discover that it was a breech birth, tail-first.

We needed to act fast. So Kent and Quentin pulled with all their might and there came a horrible squelching sound. I thought, "Shit, they've pulled the legs off!" Then came an even worse stench and a gush of slime. It was necrotic placenta, one of the more disgusting substances you can imagine. The calf had been dead inside its mother for about three days. It was a vile scene, but the worst of it was that the slime flew through the air and hit poor Quentin right in the face. I saw him open his mouth and I screamed, "Quentin! Whatever you do, don't lick your lips!" He froze. Quentin was a hunter and a woodsman, but he turned a shade of green I didn't think existed in nature and lost his battle with his gag reflex.

So the calf died, we had to put Crystal down, and I was feeling unspeakably dismal. A quarter of a bottle of brandy later, things were more bearable. Then Kent walked in and said with zero irony, "Ready for dinner?" And we actually changed out of our slimy clothes, washed our hands, and went. Quentin, to his credit, still came around to see Becky for some time, but he learned never to wear shorts and flip-flops to our house around calving time, and for some strange reason he never got close to the barn.

CHAPTER FOURTEEN

Kid Stuff

Children and animals have a relationship that is like nothing else. It's almost symbiotic: the animals accept being turned into dolls, tea party hostesses and riding mules while the children treat them with utter wonder and reverence. I was that way as a child, when the creature bug first affixed itself to my jugular vein and began pumping farmer's wife venom into my body. I remember when I was three and my family was living in South Africa, someone asked me what I wanted to be when I grew up. It's perhaps my earliest memory. Well, I wanted to be a farmer's wife. Ironically, we moved around so much that we never had pets. So you have this kid who had read every animal book in the library and was certifiably animal-crazed, but who had no animals.

I would spend hours talking to cows that roamed on a neighbor's farm. I would bring them carrots and grass. I would crawl like a Marine in boot camp under the barbed wire fence so I could stand in the field. I was so desperate to communicate with animals that I'm sure my parents thought I was dangerously unbalanced.

We had a stray cat that would come onto the property. I would follow it all day to try to learn how to walk without making a sound. I was the kid who wanted to walk everyone's dog. I would look after them. I didn't care what kind or which one. It's like couples who can't have a child. It's hard to explain.

Eventually, I got my first pet. Now, I know what you're thinking—kitten, hamster, maybe a rabbit. No. Even then, I disdained the ordinary and sensible in favor of the potentially hilarious. My first pet was—wait for it—a caterpillar. I found him when I was seven years old. He was brown with banana-colored stripes, and while I don't remember what his name was, he was unspeakably cute with his scrunchy little body and tickly legs.

Well, Mr. Caterpillar went everywhere with me. He liked to eat the little tiny apples that fell off the tree in our yard. We had a very large garden back in those days—about three acres—but when you're seven years old, you get that space dilation effect that makes three acres seem like 40. I could get lost all day in our yard; I would find myself in this *Dandelion Wine* zone of trees and wind whispering over tall grass, where space and time break down. When we become adults, most of us lose the ability to go to that place. I think that's sort of sad.

I would literally carry my caterpillar around with me all day, and at night he would sleep in his little glass jar. It seemed to me like I had him forever (that child's timelessness at work again), but in reality it was more like two weeks. So when I couldn't find him one day, I was devastated. I looked everywhere—I don't think I sank to the depths of crawling around on my hands and knees calling, "Here, caterpillar,

caterpillar, caterpillar," but I can't be sure—but he was nowhere to be found.

Then I went to the bathroom in the middle of the night and felt something *crunch* underneath my foot. I was seized with dread, mixed with a little bit of twisted child's curiosity about what the body fluids might look like as they leaked out. I lifted up my foot and saw my caterpillar squished into oblivion by my oafishness. It was horrible! I had committed lepidoptercide. It was my first experience of true loss of a pet. After that, I swore off any critters that could be mistaken for the poop of a larger creature. I figured I needed pets that at least fought back when I tried to kill them.

Bilbo Baggins

Bilbo Baggins was my first non-caterpillar pet. It was my 16th birthday, and I had my first job at an animal shelter in England. Every morning, I would cycle five miles to be at work by 6 a.m. It was heaven for an animalholic like me. Once I got to the shelter, one of my responsibilities was to clean out the run where injured seagulls would be brought and treated. The shelter had this vicious seagull, sort of the tyrant-in-residence, who couldn't fly but could run at tremendous speed flapping its wings at you. It was quite effectively terrifying. The bloody bird knew you were scared, so it would make your life a misery. I don't know if you've seen a seagull beak up close and personal, but it is perfectly capable of drilling a hole through your hand.

The first time I met this wicked bird, I was completely intimidated. It was okay when I was outside the runs; I was wearing rubber Wellingtons and carrying a big broom and felt quite important. But the Satanic gull would hide and ambush me as I came in. He would wait for me every morning and attack as soon as I got off my bike. He also knew when I didn't have on my tough-mama boots. Whoever came up with the term "bird brain" has never been ambushed and attacked by a terrorist seagull. I don't remember his name, either, but let's just call him Jonathan Livingston bin Laden.

Anyway, back to my sixteenth birthday. I decided that the only way to get a pet was to present a *fait d'accompli* to my parents. Otherwise, they would bring up the same excuse they always did: we were always moving. But I didn't give a shit anymore: I wanted something furry to share my bed. So along came Bilbo, who was a gift from my friends. He was a tan and white hamster that I took everywhere with me.

Well, not long after Bilbo joined our clan, the other reason Mum and Dad didn't allow me a pet reasserted itself: I tended to lose track of them. Mr. Baggins disappeared into the depths of our two-story house. My parents weren't too happy about having an escaped rodent within the house. Hamsters can disappear into little holes, chew through electrical cables or die behind the wallpaper leaving a nasty smell. I figured at least I wasn't likely to flatten this pet with a crunch while searching in the dark, but that was small consolation.

I spent the whole day looking for him. Finally, by chance, I went into a cupboard in the formal dining room, which I don't think I'd opened in the six months we'd been in the house. There was Bilbo curled up into a tiny little ball on the cold linoleum—not a place a hamster would typically be. So why had my stupid hamster hung out there, of all places?

Next to him was the answer: a box of liquor-filled candy. He had devoured two of them. Bilbo was dead drunk! I could see it in his sluggish little nose, his red eyes and his clumsy movements.

I learned two things that morning. First, Bilbo was lucky to be alive. Second, Bilbo was not a happy drunk. He turned into "Psycho-Hamster," so vicious when I touched him that he fell over backwards. So what does one do with a hammered hamster? I did what anyone would do when a friend has had a few too many: I carried him to his cage so he didn't have to walk or drive. He didn't move for a full 24 hours. When he did poke his head out of the fluff, his eyes were black slits filled with pain. The burning question of whether hamsters get hangovers had finally been answered. They do.

Like his hobbit namesake, Bilbo liked to have adventures. Three months into his life with us, he developed a huge abscess on his shoulder. This thing grew and grew like something from a 1950s monster movie. I was still working at the shelter, where a vet came by every few days or so. I told the vet that I had a hamster that had a growth, and I asked what it would cost to bring him in to be looked at. Now, I worked 12 hours a day, six days a week for five pounds a week. The vet told me that it cost 15 pounds for an examination and 50 pounds for the surgery. That was a whole summer's pay!

I'm a sucker for any animal, and putting Bilbo to sleep, as some of my co-workers suggested, was out of the question. My only major hurdle was getting the hamster to the clinic on my bike. I thought about putting him in my pocket, but what would I do if he jumped out while I was riding? I got an old-fashioned top zip plastic shopping bag from my mother, put him in the bottom and zipped him in. There was no way for him to jump out, and the bag fit nicely on my bike basket. So I cycled my five miles, feeling quite self-satisfied with my ingenuity. Of course, my nemesis, the Seagull of Doom, was waiting for me. I was totally preoccupied with kicking the rotten bird away from the bag without losing my balance on the bike, and when I finally did open the bag, there was no hamster!

"Oh my God!" I thought. "I've killed another friend!" Somewhere along my five-mile route, I figured my hamster was lying flattened in the road. I looked around me. Nothing. I checked my pockets to no avail. I even got close enough to bin Laden to make sure that Bilbo wasn't dangling from his beak. Nothing. Then I lifted the shopping bag out of the basket and saw Bilbo hanging like something out of the Cirque de Soleil from the bottom of the bicycle basket by one arm. He must've had forearms like Popeye, because it looked like he had traveled a considerable distance like at great speed. His expression said simply, "Get me the fuck off this thing, would you please, and keep that homicidal bird at a distance while you're at it?"

Bilbo had his surgery and did extremely well, and it curtailed his escapes. Like all good teenagers I vowed never to leave him behind…then I left him behind with my parents when I traveled to London. When I returned four months later, I learned that he had passed on and left the premises with the garbage. Bilbo Baggins stands out in my mind not only as my first pet, but also as a survivor. I still don't know how he did it.

The Great Bunny Caper
I've tried never to lie to my children about the realities of life on a farm. Animals die, sometimes quite suddenly, often quite gruesomely. It's a fact of farm life. But there was one time when I tried to soften the blow and got much more than I bargained for in the weird, quasi-mystical way that seems to be a regular part of my life.

Many years ago, we got Becky this floppy-eared bunny that she named Lu. It developed impacted teeth that turned into abscesses, and it was bye-bye bunny. Rabbits are notoriously difficult to treat. So we got Lu Two. Lu Two didn't do so well, either, and after a short time, while Becky was away at school, she expired. I thought, "My God! What am I going to tell this child who is probably seven or eight?" Losing two pets in such a short span of time can be really traumatic. So I decided to make the situation even worse by doing something really stupid.

I found a bunny with identical markings and the same age. I passed this one off as Lu Two. It didn't have the same personality at all. In fact, he was much nicer! This went on for about three weeks. Becky kept saying, "Lu Two is so much nicer now." Another difference was that Lu Two was a female and the replacement was a male. We hadn't done that close of an inspection. Oops.

Eventually, I couldn't keep the lie going any longer. I can remember going into the bathroom, putting the seat down, sitting on the toilet, bursting into tears and telling my daughter that Mommy had done a terrible thing. "Mommy lied to you," I sobbed. "That's not your Lu Two!" She took it pretty well, in part because this bunny turned out to be the most awesome bunny I've ever met.

His real name was Cappuccino. He was one of those bunnies that had free reign of the house, and he used this dictatorial power to herd the cats. Rabbits will do that. He would collect the cats from all over the house, herd them into a circle, then run circles around them. The poor cats, who just wanted to be left alone to shred the draperies and perhaps maim a field mouse or two, sat there with an expression that said, "What the bloody hell is this? I should be killing this fur ball, shouldn't I?" The sodding rabbit would even use the cats' litter box, which in my opinion is really pouring salt in the wound.

Two years later Cappuccino went into kidney failure. The vet tried to put in fluids through a catheter in the vein in his ear, but Becky said it wasn't fair to prolong his life like that. Even at a young age, she understood that death is a part of life and sometimes, a merciful and loving part. She held her rabbit in her lap when they put him to sleep, and afterwards we put him in a box so we could take him home to bury him on the farm. All animals have a place on the farm, whether it's above ground or below it. I know the resting place of every creature who's died on this farm. I figure that's the least I owe them.

After this latest pet was planted in the earth, my daughter said that only wish she'd made was that she be sent another Cappuccino. Now, let me get into something that may make some of you roll your eyes and slam this book shut thinking, "Great, another woo-woo wacko." Try to resist, because this really is something. All my life, especially when it comes to animals, amazing coincidences and astonishing synchronicities that can only be called "intention fulfillment" have swirled around me. It's uncanny. I have always been attuned to animals and their wellbeing as a healer, energy sensitive and someone who loves them, but the universe has also brought me some of the most amazing gifts—gifts I wasn't even sure I had asked for. That's what happened here.

Cappuccino had rather unusual coloring: a beautiful thick white fur with cappuccino-colored spots all over him. It wasn't a coat you would run across every day. Well, one day Becky went off to feed the pig, the horse, and all the other animals, and suddenly I heard her screaming! I bolted. We'd had a problem with pygmy rattlesnakes in the area and I thought she'd seen one, or worse. But when I got there, panting and panicked, she said, "Mommy, look!" Sitting in the middle of the pasture was a tiny, three-week-old version of Cappuccino. Now, you tell me, how did THAT happen?

The only thing we could think of it that Cappuccino had gotten out of his cage and gotten busy with a wild female rabbit. He was tame like a dog, and he had the run of the farm, so he could have gone anywhere he wanted to. It's not inconceivable he could have grabbed a few scented candles, some bunny Barry White and gone and done the nasty with some long-eared tramp in the bushes. So that this tiny rabbit had been born wasn't supernatural.

But...wild bunnies don't come out to play in broad daylight. Especially when they're weeks old. If they do, anything from a fox to a hawk will kill and devour them in no time. Yet this one did, and it ended up in the middle of our pasture. How? Then it let my daughter just walk over and pick it up. Looking closer, we could see that he had nearly the exact same coffee coat markings as his presumptive daddy. That bunny was named Miracle for obvious reasons. And became part of the family. Becky had her wish.

It's a funny thing, but when one of the animals at the farm passes, another always takes its place. I don't mean that literally; you can't replace that specific animal. But maybe they come back as a piggy, stroll around the farm, get fed, and have an occasional panic attack in the middle of a field. They may want to come back. It's not a bad life. We tell our clients that death may, in fact, just be the end of a phase.

CHAPTER FIFTEEN

Diva, the Special Needs Turkey

I know that I've already shared the story of Susannah, the special needs chicken, so please don't think that I set out deliberately to take on the care of fowl that are challenged. It just sort of works out that way. I attract strange animal-related happenings; it's both blessing and curse. But with Diva, it was different. Every animal that enters our lives is special in one way or another, but then along comes a creature that takes over your life and pulls at your heartstrings. Into my cynical, "no animal is going to get the best of this girl" life came Diva.

I'm not sure how or why I ended up with the turkey in the first place. Frankly, turkeys can be scary if they don't like you. Shouting "Thanksgiving!" doesn't seem to deter them any if they have decided to be mad at you. They display their tails, expand their wattle (that scrotum-like wrinkly thing under their chins) and go beet red with anger, just before the attack is launched. But that is just the *males*, and we all know that males will put on all kinds of embarrassing displays if they think it will get them laid. Tom turkeys shake their wattles; male humans wear Hawaiian shirts and Axe body spray. I fail to see the difference. Boys will be boys.

Female turkeys are, well, different. They are a little bird brained. They are not known for spending the afternoon toying over a Sudoku puzzle. In fact, the two females we inherited from the petting zoo actually drowned themselves by holding their heads up to the heavens, opening their beaks wide and inhaling while the heaviest possible central Florida rain fell.

No, that story is not a myth. Turkeys really are that dumb, or they are psychologically disturbed to the point of suicide.

Apparently, this sort of splendidly brainless behavior is very common with the white turkeys that are normally associated with dinner. These birds would never normally make it to the dizzy age of one year old, as they are bred to mature quickly and develop large breast muscles as soon as they can. The better to eat you with large helpings of mashed potatoes and cranberry sauce, my dear. As Kurt Vonnegut would say, so it goes.

Meeting Diva

Diva started off as a cute, oversized bird that needed a heat lamp and safe surroundings, so of course she spent the first few weeks of her life in the place where all challenged creatures end up: my shower. This is the same shower—adjoining my daughter's bedroom—that over the years has housed deer, calves, chickens, rabbits, guinea pigs, one sexually aroused chimp…pretty much anything that required extra TLC.

As I mentioned, turkeys grow quickly and soon Diva became a chicken on steroids: long legs, long neck and a perpetually bug eyed look that one generally associates either with thyroid disease or the late Marty Feldman. I had underestimated the bonding process in the early shower days and it soon became apparent that she regarded me as either:

a) Her mommy
b) Her fearless turkey leader, or
c) Her mate, in a lesbian turkey kind of way

It was hard to tell which thought might pass through her brain in any given millisecond (there was only room for one at a time). But the bonding was mutual. She was a good companion. When I was doing yard work she was always eager to help turn over leaves and look for yummy bugs underneath, and always ready to make her special little noises when she greeted me. I learned never to underestimate the friendship of a turkey.

Then one day I looked at the teenage Diva and thought I noticed teenage acne. This was weird (a phrase that should be on my family crest, I think). The top of her head was breaking out in rather revolting pustules. Now, the great thing about being married to a vet is that when your chickens or turkeys get sick and you *finally* get through that you really are seriously asking a medical question, there is always a sharp intake of breath, and you know that the only time they have seen this condition it was a) untreatable or b) you wouldn't bother anyway. Realistically of course, with turkeys being raised by the thousands in factory conditions, any weakness is just culled off, as a problem of this order can wipe out a whole flock.

After taking a good look at Diva, Kent pronounced it a severe case of turkey pox. No, that is not a joke. There really is such a thing. Now it does have some long Latin gobbledygook (pardon the pun) name to identify it but basically Diva had a severe case of staph infection that was spreading rapidly throughout her body.

Never daunted by such a prognosis, we took her to the clinic where we cultured the yucky, oozing sores and sent the sample off for a full analysis so we could determine which antibiotic might work. By now her emerging feathers were breaking as soon as they tried to emerge and the pox had spread all over her body. Everyone thought she looked disgusting. Not me. I knew we would get her to turn into a swan if we just tried hard enough. We bathed her with special shampoos daily, injected her with antibiotics and after a few weeks she became, not quite a candidate for "Ultimate makeover" but pretty darn close, I thought.

As you can imagine, during this time she lost all sense of being a turkey and considered herself as one of the family. She loved to sit out on the patio with us as we watched the sun setting, sipping wine while she enjoyed an ice water. I only had to move and she would be by my side in an instant. You could never have wanted for a more faithful companion. So when, I arose from the chair one day and turned around to see her fall over I knew something was very wrong. The joints in her legs seemed swollen and one of her legs was at an odd angle.

Once again, my friendly veterinarian was consulted and I was told that this was also very common in this breed; these turkeys were designed to grow huge breasts and then be eaten. Living far past her intended lifespan, she had gained too much weight for her legs. She was a victim of man's genetic interference. There was no surgery we could do, no medications; she was doomed to be a cripple.

Life With Diva

In time, Diva and I got used to her ambulatory difficulties. We would walk slower around the farm. I would pick her up from a sitting position until she could walk, until the day when she became a total paraplegic. It's easy to see why most people would say I should have put her to sleep, but she still enjoyed life. She liked to spread her wings out on the grass and let the ants run over them as they secreted nature's finest pesticide to kill off skin mites.

She liked to nibble the grass by her feet, and of course she liked to watch TV, though we never let her watch anything that might upset her delicate turkey sensibilities, like the Food Network. She lived in the shower full-time. She had her own little pink camouflage bed, with *Diva* printed in sparkly silver letters. She had a heat lamp at night if the air conditioner was too cold, and she was very happy in her personal space. She even was willing to share. A little cat named Mouse, who was also lame, would sleep in the bed with her every night. They were the best of friends.

Of course, she shared her domain with all the people who decided to use that toilet. It was hilarious. You could guarantee that someone would go in there, take care of business, and come out to announce, with great amazement, "Did you know that you have a *turkey* in your shower?"

"Really?" I would sometimes deadpan. Did they think that she got there on her own? It was always good for ensuring at least one non-return guest. Then came the questions, mainly about the housekeeping aspect. So, to set the record straight, Diva had her bed lined with doggy pads, in case of any accidents, but the reality was she would last for hours with never a mess. She would wait until I lifted her out into the yard, holding her up with my hands so that she cleared the ground, and was able to attend to business. She may have had special needs, but she was housebroken!

Every day I would put her in a flowered doggy bag, like one of those that trendy Beverly Hills Chihuahuas are carried in, and take her to work. We went everywhere together. Walks with the dog, out to the park. I wanted her to experience the joys of being outside looking at the world going by. As I mentioned before, she loved watching TV. I would put her special bed next to the dog's on the floor and she would spend a peaceful family evening surrounded by cats, dogs and her human friends.

I couldn't eat turkey, needless to say, and I haven't since. Not for Thanksgiving, not for Christmas. Never. In fact, at one point a local TV station was going to do a segment on the only turkey that was going to be at the table as opposed to *on* it. But it wasn't to be. After about six months of full-time nursing and love, the paralysis seemed to spread and my Diva developed pneumonia. We struggled for days as she ran a high fever and was unable to eat. We gave her fluids, antibiotics, force-fed her to get her nutrition and I thought we had it beaten the day she took a little food from my hand, making the special noise she always greeted me with. I picked her up and gave her a cuddle and saw her little eyes close, as she gave a little sigh and she passed onto the next journey.

So don't let me hear you insulting someone by calling them a turkey. I shall consider you to be insulting one of my best buddies.

CHAPTER SIXTEEN

Hellshire Farm

You've really got to watch yourself when I ask you to do something. I've already mentioned the misleading "fencing party." Well, one of the fundamental truths about life that Kent and I have discovered is that you can get an aspiring veterinarian to do just about anything if you promise that it will give him or her "valuable experience in dealing with animals."

Well, the time came when we wanted to increase the number of cattle in our herd for tax purposes, to keep the grass down, and supply us with food. We were down to about nine cows when we really wanted 20 or more. So one day Kent and I looked at each other and said, "We need to buy some cows."

There's a great little magazine called the *Florida Market Bulletin*. Through it, we eventually found these cattle down south in a town we'd never heard of, so Kent called the guy, who spoke only Spanish. We had staff members translate for us, and it was decided that we'd set off about 4PM on Friday after work. We figured we'd be home by 7PM. We invited Jorge, a technician working for us (and an aspiring veterinarian, so we knew we could manipulate him). But as we were hitching up the cattle trailer to set off for the journey, we got a bad omen: we had to swap fuses to get the truck running, which meant we would have to be without either the windshield wipers or the radio. This being Florida, where the skies can open at any time, I chose to keep the wipers. Me being me, I assumed this was a signal that we should not even start on this journey. Sadly, I was right.

Beam Me Up, Kent
We got about ten miles down the road and were trying to program our destination into the GPS. This was another clue that we were about to enter the Twilight Zone. The GPS kept telling us we would reach our destination in *three and a half hours*.

Now, I think my husband was a Star Trek character in another life, because he believes that we will be transported places. There's just leaving and arriving, no traveling. He had told me this was going to be a 45-minute drive; clearly, that was not to be the case. Fifteen minutes after we left, the clouds broke apart and the rain came down like ball bearings. So as we headed south, the only thing darker than the thunderheads was my mood.

We decide to call our doctor, who is in the Army Reserves and tends to go to desolate places in Florida for training exercises. Unfortunately, he verified that if we put the pedal to the metal, we might be able to get to the ranch in two-and-a-half hours. Very reassuring. For the first hour and a half we talked about the scenery until we reached the heart of Florida. We were nearing Sebring, true country. Sebring is not the place for me. It consists of two barbecue restaurants and a church. But it's a metropolis compared to where we were heading another 30 minutes on. The closer we got, the more my voice took on a "Please don't make me live here" tone.

Each little town had three options for entertainment: a barbecue joint, a church and some kind of strip club. Do the people who live in these desolate places do a *pas de trois* on weekends? To the BBQ first, then the strip joint, then church to pray for forgiveness for ogling whatever kind of woman would strip in a town right out of *Deliverance*? I really didn't want to know.

Hellshire Farm

We had already called ahead to the gentleman to tell him we were coming and to have the cows ready. Thank God for GPS because there was nothing else out there to indicate where to go or in what direction we were going. All of a sudden, on both sides of us appeared pastures probably 2,000 acres in size, with hundreds of cattle standing in swampland. Some of the cows were standing in swamp up to their ankles, others up to their bellies.

Eventually we saw a triangular sign advertising, in English and Spanish, cows, lambs, pigs, ducks and chickens for sale. This had to be the place.

On the property was a broken down trailer that, despite my aching bladder, did not tempt me in the least. Standing next to it was a gentleman with no shirt, a stomach that would make Mr. Piggy proud, shorts, socks and shoes, and no teeth. I don't know if it's an alien abduction thing—people out here get abducted and have their teeth removed—but everybody in the sticks seems to have a mouth like a blighted building with broken windows.

The man muttered something to Jorge, who translated and said that we just needed to carry on walking back into the property to see the cows. On one side was a little shed, and inside, hanging from a bar, were these bleeding haunches of pork which clearly had been pigs a few minutes earlier. Opposite this and in full view were the pigs, so I guess they got to see what their fate was to be. There were also ducks and sheep crammed into these little pens, I presume to be ultimately consumed as well. I've never seen so much shit in my life. I really can't describe the smell to you. It's a good thing this book isn't scratch and sniff. I immediately dubbed the place Hellshire Farm. I felt like we'd arrived on the set of *Mad Max Beyond Thunderdome*.

Stampede

I had promised Jorge that this would be an experience. Suddenly I realized it was going to be more of an experience than any of us could've imagined. As we walked, I came to realize that there were no cows. It was a little puzzling. Jorge asked the farmer, "Where are the cows?" The man gave one of those infuriating shrugs and indicated that normally the heifers came up on their own to be fed. Tonight they hadn't. Oh well.

Kent was getting a little irritated and the farmer sensed that. He said that he had some young heifers and steers in a smaller pen. I declined to go in, missing my chance to wade through ankle-deep cowshit, something I normally do with gusto. So Kent was in this pen with younger animals charging all about and decided they looked quite nice. Me? I was ready to take the next bus out of the Twilight Zone and back to the world where people had full sets of choppers.

Then the farmer suggested that Kent get on an old rickety golf cart accompanied by an old Australian cattle dog that we were told was the best working dog in Florida. Jorge and I watched with equal parts bemusement and trepidation as Kent and Señor Slaughterhouse disappeared into his 1000-acre pasture. Well, it turned out that the "best working dog" was only good for chasing cattle to the farthest point in the field and making them stampede. The sun was about to set, time was marching on, and the cattle were rumbling in a huge circle, clearly not about to let anyone get close to them. This was turning into what livestock experts call a "cluster fuck."

Pizza Slut

Finally, I was ready to surrender. I suggested that maybe we should get something to eat and regroup. Our host said there was a restaurant three minutes down the road. Thirty minutes later, we arrived at the only restaurant within 100 miles, a pizza place in a strip mall where only two storefronts were not vacant. But my main concern was not so much the pizza place but my bursting bladder: at that point I would have sprinted into any building that wasn't actively on fire.

Entering, we were greeted by a woman I shall call The Hostess with the Mostest Ass. She had, cheeks down, the largest ass I have ever seen. She led us to a table, and...let me set the stage for you, shall I? This was one of those places where you walk in and all conversations cease as every head swivels to stare at you. I guess it's big news when someone new comes to town on a Friday night in Gingivitis or Rimjob or whatever the place was called. Everyone stopped eating and gave us the once over. It was like a Stephen King novel. The only three cops in the whole area were in there, each with an ass larger than the hostess. I had landed on Ass Planet. I found myself praying that the big ass disease was not contagious.

The hostess saw my desperate bladder dance and directed me to an outbuilding beyond a corridor. I've been to Las Vegas when it's 120 degrees outside, and it was nothing like the heat in this corridor. I wasn't sure if I could make it there and back without having heatstroke. But by using my sheer will to survive, I made it back to our table, at which point a waitress (with an enormous ass) asked me if I'd like something to drink. I realized that the only way to get through this was to get drunk. I ordered a beer, and she looked absolutely horrified. "We don't serve alcohol here," she said indignantly.

Fuck. I could not imagine living out in that wasteland without alcohol. If I lived in that town, I'd be a bloody alcoholic.

I swore under my breath and ordered a glass of water. Then I started looking around the restaurant and suddenly realized that all the women in the restaurant had larger asses than any cow we'd seen that afternoon. I started laughing. The food came and we were enjoying our pizza (which was actually not too bad) when The Hostess with the Mostest Ass decided to do a Gordon Ramsay and come around to see how we were enjoying our meal.

She came up and squeezed her wobbling body between our chairs, jostling us with her love handles. She leaned all her weight on the table (which must have been bolted ten feet down into bedrock to not tip over under that stress) with both hands, looked at Jorge's pizza, and said, "Hmm, you got the white pizza. Not what I would have gone for." Then she flitted (read: rumbled) to the next table, where I heard her say, "Chicken wings? Had a bad case of food poisoning from those last week."

By this time, we just wanted to leave. Kent and I walked out a bit ahead. But our hostess apparently had other ideas. The next thing we knew, feet were running up behind us and passing us. It was Jorge in a full-blown panic. "Just hurry up!" he shouted. "We have to get out of here now!"

Apparently, Her Majestic Assness had sidled up to Jorge, grabbed his arm (he was holding his box of white pizza) and suggested that his "pizza would taste very nice in the morning with some scrambled eggs on top." Jorge is a Seventh-Day Adventist and rather sheltered, so I think he was finding an outing with us to be more than he bargained for.

Cow Creeps

We set off back the 15 miles back to the farm. It was now pitch black outside. There were no lights of any kind. I was trying to explain to Kent that I really didn't think this was a good idea because these weren't really tame cattle but wild beasts. It has taken us years to get our herd to the point where we can handle every animal. But Kent was a man on a mission. Trouble was, the farm was dark and deserted. Now it felt like we had walked into a movie starring Jason or Freddy or one of those unkillable killers.

We had just the headlights of the truck to find our way to the corral, where the farmer finally managed to herd some of these irritable cows. But all we had to look at them with was a penlight, and it was causing these little beasties to stampede up and down. So we were looking at dark cows in the dark night. Finally, even Kent saw the light (pardon the pun) and said this was ridiculous. "We're going to the trailer and pulling out of here really fast before anyone sees us," he said.

We started walking back to the truck. Not a soul in sight. All of a sudden, I heard coughing. I looked at Jorge and he at me. We walked faster, and just as we got in the truck and closed the door, we heard a voice. The Mexican had been hiding in the bushes watching us. Jorge told him in Spanish that we didn't have any backing lights on the trailer. We would have to come back. I don't think a cattle trailer has ever turned around so fast.

As we headed down this long black road, surrounded on both sides by eerie swamps, I heard a noise like torrential rain falling—but it wasn't raining. Suddenly I realized with disgust that the sound was thousands of locusts or other flying insects committing mass suicide against the body and windows of the truck! It was the biblical plague we'd been waiting for.

Kent drove as fast as he could without driving us into a swamp. We finally arrived home about 11:30PM, at which time I pointed out to Jorge that he got a lot of large animal experience. Somehow, he failed to see the humor in the situation. Oddly, the next time we were off to pick up some livestock, Jorge had plans.

I can't imagine why.

CHAPTER SEVENTEEN

Cattle Call

A week later, Kent still hadn't given up on the cow idea. But this time, the sneaky bastard, he waited until I went to Guernsey, in England, to visit my ailing mother. Understand, I don't enjoy these journeys, but I want to pick the cows. I'm the primary feeder, and I'm concerned that I'm going to be providing nourishment to Psycho Herd.

Because of the time difference I received this message at 11PM, so I called my beloved back. This transatlantic call ended the way they usually do, with a loving, "Do whatever the hell you want."

It was about 3AM in England when I got the next text. Kent had found splendid beasties to buy, made the purchase, and loaded seven future steaks on legs onto our cattle trailer and headed back for our farm with what was surely a satisfied, "I told you so, honey" smirk on his face. He was coming up the I-4 turnpike through the empty country before one hits the ginormous clot of civilization that is the area around Disney World when—BAM! He blew a tire on the trailer.

This part of the highway is pitch black, so this was a dangerous situation. Kent didn't know where he was. But he remembered that a couple of miles back, he had passed two cops with their cars under an overpass. So he walked back to them and told them he needed to get the trailer off the road so he could call Triple A. Using everything they had learned from their public relations training, Florida's Finest told him that if he moved onto the road they would arrest him. Thanks for your help, gentlemen; go back to your donuts.

Finally, Kent called AAA, who told him that our premium membership didn't cover this. But after much cajoling, an AAA roadside assistance person drove up and found Kent (practically ran into him on the darkened highway is more like it) and said he would drive behind our trailer and flash his warning lights. Grateful for the assistance, Kent finally made it to the parking lot of a Target store. At this point, he called one of our long-suffering staff members and asked them to bring a spare tire to the Target, then dashed for the store to empty his aching bladder.

The next text I got from Kent informed me that the entire Florida state police brigade and a couple of fire engines for good measure were in the parking lot with their lights flashing. Oh God. The jig was up. The bad man had gone ahead and cleared his potential deathtrap from the road, and this temerity was going to land him in jail. With me not in the country to bail him out, Kent was certain he was doomed to spend the next night in a cell with Bubba the Gay Weightlifter. He walked back to the car prepared to be ordered on the ground, read his Miranda rights and all those other things you see on the police procedurals we watch entirely too much.

But it was just a weird coincidence. Kent never did figure out what all the commotion was about. Our staff member finally showed up with the spare tire, which was the wrong size. No matter. A couple of calls later, another staffer showed up with a spare trailer. Now, how many operations do you know of that have a *spare cattle trailer* just lying around? Score one for our eccentricity! They loaded the cattle up right there in the parking lot and Kent got home without ever becoming Bubba's boyfriend.

CHAPTER EIGHTEEN

The Pig and The Psychic

I am a firm and very rational believer in the paranormal because I've experienced it. I've told you about the miracle animals that seem to just show up in our yard. But for years, I've also had the ability to hold my hand over a sick animal's body and, by gauging the heat on my hand, locate its area of illness. Things like that have happened to me my entire life, and I cherish them.

But despite the fact that I was having one on my radio show, even I thought the idea of a pet psychic was sure to be utter rubbish. Talk about a blank check! I could see it playing out like this:

> *PSYCHIC: "Mr. Tiddles says he wishes you would stop making him lick peanut butter off your balls every Friday night."*
> *YOU (sputtering): "I do no such thing!"*

PSYCHIC: *"Well, that's what he's telling me."*

The pet can't exactly raise a paw and set the record straight, can it? So I thought the bar was set absurdly low for the pet psychic, a California woman named Laura Stinchfield. I was prepared to be nice but nothing more. But as usually happens, I was in for a surprise.

Another Drive to the Twilight Zone
Backstory: Kent made the mistake of asking me what I wanted for my birthday. Never do this. Most women of my sophistication and excellent breeding would request a diamond something-or-other, a trip to someplace where they could be waited on by obsequious, fawning cabana boys, or a day at a high-end spa.

I asked for a pig. This surprises you?

The facts were a) Mr. Piggy, Prince of Pigs, was nearing the end of his life (in fact, he passed away shortly before this book was completed) and I wanted a new porcine companion to replace my beloved boy. And b) I wanted fresh, cute, home-raised bacon. Out came the trusty *Florida Market Bulletin* and we found a Yorkshire sow who was already pregnant (it would turn out later that she was in fact not pregnant but just liked the clothes).

Pigs gestate for three months, three weeks and three days (which is rather poetic, in a way), and the babies weigh about a pound when born, compared to their mommies who might weigh 500 pounds. However, baby pigs put on weight faster than almost any other creature (though I can run a close second if I put my mind to it), so they fatten up to a healthy size and eventually to pork chop territory in no time.

Kent and I get one day off per week from the veterinary clinics, and we like to use it for some stressful activity. So off we went into some other unknown, meth-ridden part of Florida. We passed though the town where three teens were bludgeoned to death over a video game a few years ago. Lovely. Once again, AT&T abandoned us, so before my last bar disappeared I sent a text of the last cross street we passed. That way, in case we were about to be murdered and fed to pigs, at least the kids would know where to look for our killers.

I've Just Met a Pig Named Maria
We pulled our trailer into a farm with about eight Guatemalans who were there to show us their pig. Some spoke some English, and Kent was smart enough not to hand over the cash until he saw the swine firsthand. There were about 40 of the beasts in a chaotic enclosure, and Kent found the pregnant sow we had read about and liked the look of her. Thus began the circus. It's no easy job separating a 500-pound pig from its buddies, especially when she doesn't want to move. We tried to get her into a trailer with food, but pigs aren't known for being smart for nothing.

She crashed through the pen barrier and headed right for me. You don't argue about proper pig wrangling when an animal that large is headed for you: I jumped around the truck and hid behind a shed while our "pigboys" lassoed her and the real fun began. I videotaped it with my phone; the noise was indescribable, and it took six men to get this pig on the truck.

We always drive out of these places faster than we arrive, but unlike our trip to Hellshire Farm, we were leaving this godforsaken dump with our quarry. I named her Maria on the spot.

Unfortunately, Maria sunk into a deep depression and refused to eat or drink when we got her to the farm. Coincidentally, Mr. Piggy was also unhappy at the time, so when I found out about a pet psychic who was going to be in the area (and who coincidentally hailed from the same town as my co-author) I decided to have her on my local weekly radio show to give Mr. Piggy a reading.

Dazzle Shot

When psychic Laura Stinchfield joined me on my show, I mentioned the problems with Maria but gave her no additional information. Well, she told me that Maria had been in a place where she was constantly pushed and trampled, and said that Maria was very scared at night and would probably escape from her pen on our farm at night. This floored me, because unbeknownst to Laura, Maria had recently broken out of her pen at night and only calmed down when she encountered a young pig.

It turns out that on the farm where we got Maria, they used to slaughter the pigs at night. In fact, the shed where I took shelter when Maria came at me was the slaughterhouse, and it was in full view of the pigs. Maria was depressed because she assumed she was the next to be killed. She had also been in a very crowded enclosure with bigger pigs and *was* always in danger of being trampled. In the psychic medium business there's something called a "dazzle shot," which is a piece of information the psychic shares that's so accurate and specific that it floors everyone. Well, I was dazzled.

I asked Laura to please tell Maria psychically that her porcine life was safe. She would not be killed for food (her babies would become ham and sausage, but I didn't share that little tidbit). Since then, Maria has calmed down completely, eats a healthy diet, and has become a pig that we can pet. By the time you're reading this, she's probably also given birth to her first litter. She also became a bosom companion to my beloved Mr. Piggy during the last days of his life, for which I am profoundly grateful.

Next birthday, though, I am definitely asking for the goddamned cabana boy.

CHAPTER NINETEEN

The Hills Have Eyes, The Sequel

One of the most interesting things that I have learned during my tenure as the Queen of Spayed is that there are two Floridas. One is the Florida everyone knows about, the place of South Beach bikinis and West Palm Beach mansions, the Everglades and the manatee, the Jacksonville Jaguars and the Disney-Universal Axis of Parental Migraines, which rises from the flatlands not far from me in Orlando. But there is another Florida that no one outside our state will talk about. It's the Florida where the strange offshoots of *homo sapiens* reside. I know because every time I set out to do any pig-related business, I have to go to that Florida.

No one tells you this when you are setting up a pig-related enterprise as Kent and I were. Time was, you would go to the marketplace and buy a pig. Simple. Now you have to venture into places that Fox Mulder wouldn't go. The thing is, in most of the more civilized parts of the state, you aren't allowed to keep a pig in your yard, so to find a pig you have to venture into territory where strange alternate breeds of humans reside. Most pig farmers seem to be part of those odd strains of the species. I guess I'm a pig farmer myself now, so I don't know what that says about me.

What's really disturbing about all this is that even when Kent and I drive no more than 45 minutes from our home, we somehow find ourselves in sinister, glassy-eyed backwaters right out of "True Blood," where people sit on front porches all day and AT&T Wireless throws up its hands and says, "Screw it." One of our first pig-buying forays was to a rural part of central Florida well-known for having a high concentration of psychics. I don't know what that means other than that due to the pressures of the free market, you must be able to get one hell of a deal on having your tarot cards read.

No matter how close a pig farm is to our house, the directions always take forever. They're always filled with unnerving phrases like "turn left at the oak tree" and "turn right at the ivy-covered rock," which are, I suspect, designed to ensure that neither you nor anyone else will know precisely where you are. As you go down these small, unpaved roads the vegetation gets thicker and thicker while the light grows dimmer and dimmer, until the entire scene begins to feel unreal…and your imagination grows far more vivid.

So you can imagine how my fevered brain started churning when we were far down one of these windy roads and came to an iron gate. The children were lucky enough to be with us on this day, probably due to some half-assed notion like, "Hey, kids, let's go get some pigs today and see some funny people!" This is not an unreasonable idea; I have found that, much like visiting Fremont Street in the old downtown of Las Vegas, going pig shopping in the hinterlands is a tonic for one's self-esteem. Once you have been surrounded by the lame, the halt, the one-eyed and the inbred, that extra ten pounds on the hips or that awful recent haircut just don't seem quite as important.

We got out of the car. On the other side of the iron gate I saw something that still makes no sense to me: a blazing bonfire, and a bent over, wizened old man steadily feeding people's clothing into it. There was a strange smell on the air, which I believe was the 70 pigs quartered nearby.

I've said that my imagination was already on overdrive. Well, the only time I've ever seen anyone systematically burning clothing was on *The Sopranos*, so I immediately leapt to the conclusion that this was where the Florida Mafia brought stoolies and undercover cops to feed them to the pigs and then burn the evidence. I mean, don't most people just take old clothes to the thrift store?

The old man was so engrossed in his labors that he didn't notice us, which meant we were in that strange interval where we had a moment when we could have turned around, gotten back in the truck and driven away without a word. It was like the scene that always appears in movies like *Jeepers Creepers*, where the hero and heroine are poised to go into the spooky, dark house against their better judgment, and everyone in the audience is shouting, "No, you moronic ingenue! Drive away and go to White Castle instead!" Inevitably, they end up tortured, slaughtered and made into lampshades. Perhaps that's natural selection at work in our horror films.

I really didn't want to find out whether the same dynamic played out in real life. But just as we were about to listen to that internal voice, the old man noticed us. The social reflex kicked in and we said, "Hello!" Damn.

Now, when I talk about pigs, most people think about Babe. These pigs were not Babe. These resembled the critters from *Hannibal*: barely domesticated wild boars, huge and hairy with orange and black spots. They were confined to a large pen, which actually makes this more dangerous because they can get to you more easily.

The idea was that we were supposed to pick the pig of our choice, lead it into a cage in our truck and drive home singing a jolly "I'm having bacon in the morning" song. Bullshit. What really happened is that we chased those pigs around their pen for 45 minutes, at which point we didn't care which one was ideal because it was 95 degrees, we were hot and tired, and we just wanted a fucking pig.

While this was going on, in my mind I was wondering when the other shoe was going to drop and I was going to be fed to the pig and my clothing burned in the bonfire, along with my children. Would I have to watch my children being fed to the pig? It's amazing what your mind does when the only things occupying it are the curses your husband makes as he chases after a wild pig and the "Can we go home now?" whines of your progeny.

Finally, we lassoed our pig, got him on the truck and roared out of that godforsaken place. The old man and the folks who ran the pig farm had spent the entire time sniggering behind their hands at our desperate pig chase. Which, come to think of it, may have been the entire reason behind the enterprise.

Hog Heaven
That notion—that country bumpkins advertise pigs for sale for the sole purpose of watching city folk humiliate themselves chasing swine through mud and shit—got a great deal of support on a later trip. This pig-buying expedition was unusual for two reasons: it was very close to our house, and it was one of the only times we didn't return with a pig. Of course, even the fact that the farm was less than an hour from home didn't mean anything; we were going in search of swine,

and that meant we were headed right off the edge of civilization.

Off Kent and I drove into the sticks, then the sticks of the sticks. Night fell as it does in these parts where there are no streetlights: heavy and smothering. You could barely see your hand in front of your face. We turned down a dirt road (shockingly) and before us was a trailer. In front of the trailer was another bonfire (there seems to be this correlation between pigs and bonfires). Seated around this bonfire were half a dozen rednecks absolutely drunk out of their minds. Surrounding them on all sides were stacks of full and empty Bud Light cans. Oh joy.

Despite this, they insisted they had already tied up their best pig ready to be loaded onto our trailer. Could it be that easy? Sadly, no. Trusting fools that we are, we allowed the soused pig wranglers to handle the animal. Their hand-eye coordination being what it tends to be after you've drunk more beer than the crew of the U.S.S. Abraham Lincoln on shore leave, the pig quickly escaped and took off on a broken-field run around the fenced yard.

At this point, our redneck friends decided that it was up to us to corral the animal. I don't think *caveat emptor* really covers it here; I think it should be more like *bring your running shoes and a damned tranquilizer gun*. We had neither, so Kent and I proceeded to try to double-team this 400-pound hog and shepherd it into the truck.

If you know anything about pigs, you know such things can be spectacularly futile. Pigs are very fast and quick on their feet. Gayle Sayers himself would have been impressed with how the beastie changed direction on a dime and avoided my best open-field tackles. Meanwhile, this was clearly a great spectator sport for the good old boys; they cracked some more beers, sat around the fire and watched us chase this pig around and around like it was some sort of tribal dance. They were quite literally in hog heaven.

Finally, Kent and I, in a moment of perfect marital telepathy, looked at each other and said simultaneously, "Fuck this." We got in our truck without another word and drove away, leaving the rednecks and their mountain of Bud Light cans staring after us.

The Swamp Has Eyes
One of our more recent piggy adventures didn't involve buying a pig but taking Maria, our proud sow and my bosom companion after the loss of Mr. Piggy, Prince of Pigs, to mate. We had thought Maria was pregnant when we bought her. But after watching her make a nest and waiting the requisite three months, three weeks, three days, three minutes and three seconds, we had no litter of adorable future pork chops. I was craving the crackle of bacon fat between my teeth; this was simply unacceptable. I simply must get Maria knocked up, and since doing it myself was out of the question, I went online.

Fortunately, you can find anything on the Internet. I typed "pig mating" into Google, and after wading through some seriously disturbing video clips of sexual activity involving only *one* pig, found what I was after at PigHarmony.com or something: a healthy male pig ready for action. The farm was even close to the house; I figured we could leave at 4 p.m. and be home by 6.

The only troubling thing was that the farm was in a tiny town called Paisley. If there's a serial killer or other lunatic on the loose in central Florida, they always end up in Paisley. It's like a law of nature. The town of about 750 people is the East Coast distributorship for psychopathy. And that's where Kent and I were headed on Pig Quest 2010.

Initially, the trip was a breeze. I had spent days training Maria to follow a trail of food into her cage and lie down, and come the day she was to meet her suitor, she performed flawlessly. Maria seemed to enjoy the wind between her ears as we drove along.

You always know when the directions to a place include the words, "Go until the road ends, and then keep going" that you're in trouble. The deeper we went into the uncharted Central Florida wilderness, the lower the coverage bars on my iPhone went. As is my practice, before we lost our precious cellular signal entirely, I made one last call to the clinic. It's always a good idea to let someone know where you are, because they will know where to send the search party when you don't come back.

We are graced by a wonderful receptionist, a Puerto Rican lady named Chiqui. Apart from her exemplary qualities as an employee, she also happens to be quite renowned for her psychic abilities. When I told Chiqui where we were, not being one to keep anything to herself, she said in her thick Latin accent, "Oh, no, I have a bad feeling about this place. You must promise me you will leave before the sun goes down."

After a pause, I had to restrain myself from snapping, "Well, why the fuck didn't you say something before we left?" But Chiqui really is a dear, so I refrained. I promised her we would escape before the sun went down and the vampires emerged to feast on our blood, and she went off to light candles or whatever it is psychics do. But now I was thoroughly spooked. I have had many psychic experiences and put a great deal of stock in Chiqui's pronouncements. I told Kent about what she said and he shrugged. In for a penny, I supposed. We kept driving.

As we chugged further and further into the wilderness, the trail we drove on became narrower and narrower.

Refrigerators and couches began to appear by the side of the road. In looked like the inside had come outside. Then I started to notice that on many of the old, broken-down couches sat people. There were dozens of people just perched on decrepit, moldy furniture in the middle of fields, without a house in sight, watching us as we passed. I swore I could hear banjos in the background.

I grabbed Kent's arm. "It's like *The Hills Have Eyes*," I hissed. He kept his eyes on the road and we went on.

We got lost and made a couple of U-turns (not easy with a trailer and a large pig) and all the while I was sure I could see movement out of the corner of my eye—shapes like people ducking behind trees as we drove by. I was hoping that we ended up at the right place the first time, because all I had to do was look at the Confederate flags, the mountains of discarded beer cans, and the carcasses of burned out and rotting cars strewn everywhere to know that this was a place where they shot first and asked questions later.

Eventually, we arrived at our chosen destination, and the first words out of my mouth were, "Oh my God, Kent, it looks like a tornado came through here." It really did, with the lot half filled with huge piles of metal roofing and blocks of concrete. Turns out that a tornado had come through back in 2007, but they hadn't got around to cleaning up. The owner was kind enough to point out the remains of their old trailer sitting in the branches of a tree across the road. Since then, the human residents had been living in a FEMA trailer.

A young, barefoot boy came out to meet us enthusiastically, and I was certain that I could hear the distant twang of "Dueling Banjos." He seemed overly happy to see people and proudly showed us around the small farmstead. The animals were in surprisingly good condition and enjoyed considerably better quarters than their human keepers.

Then...there he was. In all his glory. Maria's future husband. Violins swelled and played the theme from *Love Story*. He was an impressive specimen who was also sporting a very impressive piece of manly equipment. Goodness. I ogled it for a moment, and then decided not to mention anything to Kent. Men can be so insecure, you know.

His owner was a nice young woman who had been very involved in 4H, and she seemed to know her business. But I wasn't sure about leaving Maria here. We had bonded over the recent weeks, and I wasn't sure how she would react to being left out here where it took six people to round up a full set of teeth. The young boy put his hand into her pen and I was sure he was going to get his fingers eaten, but apparently he was some sort of pig whisperer or pig savant. Maria just sniffed him placidly.

Okay, I thought, time to stop being superstitious and get this done. I got Maria down the ramp from her cage and to the pen to meet her new friends and her macho man.

Then I noticed that the sun was sinking toward the horizon. The deep shadows of the dense trees were lengthening. I swore I could hear wolves howling. The young boy became more effusive in talking to us. *He's trying to delay us*, my fevered mind thought as my superstitions came roaring back. I heard Chiqui's words, "You must promise to leave before the sun goes down." I promised God and the Universe that if we got out of this, I would consult with our Puerto Rican receptionist before I did so much as go to the store for milk.

I hustled Kent into the truck, said my quick goodbyes to Maria, and jumped in. Despite the fact that the strange boy was running beside our truck jabbering a mile a minute, we floored it and got back onto the trail through the woods. I noticed that what I had thought to be woods was actually a swamp filled with ghostly trees and dead automobiles. Then—

right there! I definitely saw it: people ducking behind the trees just out of sight.

"This isn't *The Hills Have Eyes*," I said to Kent, who was getting a little jumpy himself now despite his Midwestern pragmatism. "This is the sequel, *The Swamp Has Eyes*."

The sky was growing darker and darker. It occurred to me that to whoever—or whatever—inhabited those swamps, a 2005 Chevy Avalanche would probably be a very nice addition to their graveyard of cars. We were swerving and fishtailing on this sandy road as Kent tried to go as fast as he could without putting us in a watery grave.

I don't know what I was thinking. I was half-convinced we were going to end up as some sort of anti-tornado sacrifice. Scenes from *The Blair Witch Project* played out on the movie screen of my mind. Then—we hit tarmac. Hallelujah. Kent and I looked at each other and saw our future. He floored the gas…

…and a truck suddenly pulled from a driveway in front of us and completely blocked the road. *Oh my God. This is it*, I thought. They had us trapped. Now the sun would go down and the things behind the trees would shape shift and come and get us. We would never see Maria or our kids again! I would miss the birth of my first grandchild! I would never have the chance to wring Chiqui's neck for failing to warn us before we left!

We sat there in our standoff with the truck. Then, just as the last rays of sun were vanishing from the sky, the driver (if there was one) reversed and cleared the road. You have no idea how fast an Avalanche can accelerate when it has to.

**PART THREE:
CLINICALLY INSANE**

CHAPTER TWENTY

Underwear A La Carte

About ten years ago a gentleman came into the clinic with Buster, a male Doberman around twelve years old. We had taken care of this man's dog for several years, but we had always been reluctant to go in the exam room while he was still at the clinic because he always seemed to find an excuse to talk about underwear. It was the oddest thing. Well, we were about to find out why.

When he brought Buster in, the poor dog was not doing very well, and the man confessed that it was probably because the dog had eaten a pair of his red silk boxer shorts. This is actually not unusual. Dogs will eat just about anything—knives, tennis balls, fish hooks, you name it—and most dogs, after all, have extremely sensitive noses. Bloodhounds have a sense of smell that's about ten million times keener than that of a human being. So it should come as no surprise that a dog in a domestic environment, particularly one that's left alone for long periods during the day, will amuse itself by "sampling" the most aromatic objects it can reach. These are, for obvious reasons, usually dirty male or female undies.

Let's be honest, we leave some of our most interesting olfactory traces in our discarded knickers. I've heard of dogs that would chew the crotches out of women's panties and leave the rest of the fabric alone. One can almost imagine a dog bistro and a canine underwear sommelier (or would that be "smellier"?) presenting the evening's collection of fine underwear varietals to a discerning hound: "You are having zee Alpo? Excellent. I would recommend zee 2007 Maidenform cotton, pale pink, with a hint of perspiration..."

So I wasn't surprised to hear that Buster had downed some drawers. Upon examining the poor pooch, it was clear he was having some digestive troubles. He had not been eating and of course had been losing weight. Frequently, when we run into a case like this we'll feed the dog something, allow his digestive tract to do its work and try to clear the problem naturally. Once a frantic owner brought us a cat that had devoured her darning needles. Well, my brilliant husband simply fed the cat cotton balls for about a half hour (what surprised me was how willingly the cat ate them), until the needles caught on one of the balls and eventually passed out the other end, no harm done.

Obviously, that wasn't going to work with old Buster. He was in some distress, and after taking some x-rays we could see that some kind of soft object had wound itself up pretty tightly into his stomach, blocking the digestive tract, and had moved partially into the small intestine, which was causing even more problems. We told the owner that surgery would be necessary to remove the obstruction, and asked him to come back the next day to see Buster.

The surgery was pretty routine...until we found that not only did Buster have a partially digested pair of red boxer shorts in his alimentary canal, he also had a pretty old and rather disgusting pair of what were obviously Victoria's Secret ladies' panties wadded in there. No wonder the old boy was having troubles. He was a cross-eater! This gender equality might have been politically correct but it didn't do the dog any favors. But once we had the underwear out, it was easy to sew him up and get him into recovery. Then we called the owner, told him the surgery had been successful, and asked him to come by the clinic the next day to see his dog.

The next morning the gent arrived at our offices...with his wife. Thinking nothing of it, we ushered them into the recovery area where they could see Buster, who was doing fine. Kent proceeded to tell them about the surgery. "We found the boxer shorts that you told us about," he says, holding them up, "but we also found an older pair of underwear." And he held up the Victoria's Secret lingerie.

Yes, you've figured out what's coming. I could feel the temperature the room drop about twenty degrees as the husband got that rabbit-about-to-be-mashed-flat-by-a-car look. His wife's voice was icy:

"I've never shopped at Victoria's Secret."

Whoops.

I don't know the full details of what went on after that, other than they left the clinic in the midst of a heated discussion. But I do know that within a year they were divorced, and I think she got custody of Buster. My guess is that she's trained the dog to chew on men's boxer shorts with the owners still in them.

CHAPTER TWENTY-ONE

A Cloister of Monks

Many years ago, when I had been a technician at the veterinary clinic for only a week, and Kent and I were not carnally or connubially involved in any way (a situation I soon remedied by batting my fetching eyelashes), I accompanied him on a trip to euthanize the Yorkshire terrier of one of our better customers.

It may strike you as odd (as it does me) that in the veterinary profession, one of the last services you provide some of your best and most loyal patrons is to kill the creature they spent so many years relying on you to keep alive. But that's the business. Often, the final act of love we can help a pet owner perform is to let an old and crippled animal exit this life with peace and serenity. But we usually don't make house calls to do it.

However, this woman was a special case, and when she summoned us to her very posh neighborhood, we responded. So off Kent and I went on a gloriously sunny Florida day, pulling up to this fancy house. I envisioned this as a sort of James Herriot adventure, where we would do the deed and then discuss it over a crumpet or two. But when the woman answered the door, shrill bells started to clang in my head. I have since learned that this is my "crazy alarm," which forewarns me that the person in question is very likely a couple of irons short of a full golf bag and I should be on my guard.

Do you remember the television show *The Addams Family*? Well, the reason my alarm bells jangled was that our customer came to the door looking very much like Morticia Addams. Curious. Kent and I greeted her and went into the house, and it was pitch black, like going from the bright outdoors into a movie theater, where you can't see your hand before your face until your eyes adjust. Curiouser. I was tempted to quip, "What's playing and where do we get the popcorn?" but I stifled my natural smart-ass tendencies.

As my senses adjusted and our hostess led us through the house, I noticed several things in succession. First, there was so much incense burning that the Maharishi Mahesh Yogi would have said, "Can we dial that back a little?" Second, there was odd, deep chanting coming from all around us, like a group (What is a group of monks called? A gaggle? A cloister?) of monks was hiding in the pantry and laundry room. I realized that Morticia had put Gregorian chant on a surround sound system. Finally, every window in the house had been blacked out and the curtains drawn.

I hadn't known Kent or worked at the clinic that long, but I was already becoming aware that at the intersection of pets and the people who own and love them, you find some deeply strange behavior. I had already met a client who had suggested that he and Kent wife swap. This was not Kansas, Toto. Perhaps I came from a naïve background; in England, you don't generally ask the vet if he wants to screw your wife while you watch.

Morticia led us toward the back of the house. We were all speaking in low, hushed tones befitting the solemn work ahead, because after all, we were there to euthanize her dog. Finally, we emerged into the pitch-black kitchen and there found one lonely 25-watt light bulb shining down onto the kitchen table. I have an active, morbid and oft-twisted imagination, and the first bubble that popped into my conscious mind was that this looked like a perfect setup for a human sacrifice. I started to be concerned about myself. After all, Morticia wasn't going to sacrifice Kent; he was the skilled veterinarian. I was a lowly technician and thus expendable. I began to eye the exits like Jason Bourne.

"I'll go get him for you," she whispered and slipped out of the room. At that, I was relieved, because it meant I was off the hook. In a few moments, she returned with this poor ancient Yorkie, terribly sick and in pain. Many times euthanasia is an act of mercy and love, and this was clearly one of those times. This poor thing had a terrible quality of life and it was time for him to move on to the next life.

However, one of the things that makes Kent a great vet is that he always talks with the client about what is about to happen, then asks if they are ready. The question is basically, "Are you ready to kill your best friend?" This is the last chance to back out, and we have to ask because we have to know if the owner can handle it. Some people change their minds at the last minute and feel that they're doing a terrible thing.

The woman swallowed, kissed her Yorkie, nodded and backed away from the table so Kent could do his job. There were about 200 incense cones burning, so much that I could barely breathe, and the cloister of monks chanting away in the background. Frankly, I don't remember James Herriot having to go through all this shit.

It wasn't easy to find the right spot for the lethal injection in that small 25-watt light, but Kent was a true professional. He always listens to the heart even after he knows the animal is gone so he can tell the owner something: he's passed on, he's gone to a better place, dig a hole in the yard, whatever.

He handed her the body of her dog, and she suddenly put the corpse aside and threw her arms around Kent in what seemed to be an unusually close embrace. Unsure what to do, Kent hugged her back. The clinch went on, and on. Based on duration alone it had morphed from a little unusual, to lurid, to bordering on something you might pay $9.99 for on a special private channel at a hotel.

There has always been a common thread to these sorts of encounters: the women who proposition Kent or disrobe before him always do it with me watching, like I'm not even there. What does one do with oneself? Watch? Pet the dead dog? Hum along with the monks? Blow out the incense and open the fucking curtains, which seemed like the best course of action?

Kent was extremely uncomfortable. The whole thing was like a scene from a 1920s melodrama with the heroine throwing herself into the hunky hero's arms and sobbing theatrically. I'm sure it was a case of "How close can I get to the hunky veterinarian?"

Finally, after what seemed like the third round of "Ave Maria" from the cloister of monks, I chirped to Kent that we had other appointments that afternoon. He looked at me gratefully and disentangled himself from Morticia; I don't think he was quite sure we were ever going to be able to leave that house. We said our farewells and found our way to the front door. The blinding daylight felt wonderful.

As walked to the car, I was certain I could hear a group of monks singing, "Duh-duh-duh-DUM," followed by the "snap-snap" of fingers.

CHAPTER TWENTY-TWO

Chow, Baby

A lot of pet owners think that it's nicer for their pet to stay at home when they travel than to be shipped off to some sort of kennel or boarding facility, because the animal gets to stay in a familiar environment. As someone who owns a full-service pet resort, I strenuously disagree, but that's beside the point. The point is that an encounter with one of those pampered pets was one of the few instances where Kent and I actually came close to tasting Death's sweet kiss.

A Korean gentleman who lived in a very posh neighborhood, a place where ex-presidents have lived, was one of the "let the dog stay at home" crowd. When he went on a trip, he engaged the services of a female pet sitter for his chow, Baby. (A brief aside here: every chow that has ever tried to bite me has been named Teddy, because it looks like a teddy bear, or Baby, because I don't know why.)

We were in the middle of a typically busy morning at the clinic when we got a frantic call from this pet-sitting woman that the dog wouldn't let her into the house to feed it. It turned out that—and I swear this is true—that this chow would only eat Chinese food. This woman had gone out that morning to get the dog his daily orange peel chicken or something and when she came back he attacked her and, so she said, nearly killed her. She had managed to lock the dog in a screened porch enclosure, and would we be kind enough to come out and tranquilize Baby for her?

Well, shit. Apparently she couldn't reach Animal Control so we got the call. She thought the dog might be sick, because he hadn't touched the Chinese food that she'd dropped in her panicked flight. I thought it was more likely that the beast was sick from eating that crap instead of a healthy canine diet, but what the hell? Off Kent and I rode to the rescue.

When we got to this home in this very wealthy district, we saw that the woman had barricaded Baby in an area of the pool deck and anchored him to a railing made of heavy wrought iron rings. In the center was a pool whose water was such a deep fluorescent green that you couldn't see the bottom. In the middle of all this was Baby the chow, his black tongue huffing and puffing, just daring us to mess with him.

Of course, messing with him was our job, so we crept carefully into this enclosure with a catch pole, a long pole with a loop at one end that can be tightened with a quick pull—specifically made for capturing unruly critters at a safe distance and subduing them by cutting off their air. We really should have had a 22-gauge shotgun, which would have been more effective and more satisfying, but c'est la vie. Thus we attempted to lasso the dog, which is harder than it sounds, especially when said dog is trying to kill the veterinarian. Kent was doing more dodging and weaving than Muhammad Ali.

But apparently, some distant gods decided that this scenario wasn't challenging enough. What we really needed was something to make things worse! What no one realized was that the wrought iron railings the dog had been tethered to were loose. After many minutes of absorbing the energies of Baby's furious charging, one of the railings gave way. Part of one fell from above and hit me squarely on the arm. That side of my body went numb; I thought surely that I had broken my arm. But about six feet of iron railing—with the Baby the Ripper attached—fell directly on Kent and pinned him to the ground.

So here Kent was lying flat with the dog now going for his throat. I realized that when the dog sitter said that Baby had tried to kill her, she had really not been exaggerating. Kent screamed for me to get out and get back to the clinic and get some drugs—not for us, which would have been nice, but for the dog. Then, using all his upper body strength, he threw the railing and the dog off him and got to his feet. Baby, now slowed by the heavy railing, backed off temporarily.

I made the one-minute drive hyperventilating, freaking out, my arm a mess. When the staff saw me, they called the police, who came back to the house with me in case we needed to shoot the dog. The one thing we were sure of was that we could not allow Baby to escape, because it would likely kill a child.

Back at the ranch, I found Kent in a stalemate with the chow, which was now running around the edge of the pool and dragging the wrought iron railing; that shows you how strong that damned dog was. I was hoping that the dog might end up in the pool, and leading it into the water seemed like a good strategy to me, because we sure as hell weren't going into the water after it. The cops were no help; they just stood on the periphery, perhaps looking for a nearby donut shop.

Suddenly, the dog tried to run under the pool slide to get at us and rip out our throats and the railing it was dragging got caught and wedged under the slide. Now Baby was trapped, which probably saved its life, because it probably would have gone in the drink otherwise, at which point I would have found it impossible to resist an embarrassing but deeply satisfying cry of "Yes!" possibly followed by a chest bump with Kent.

Finally, Kent used a pole syringe to sedate the creature, and when Baby was unconscious, the strangest thing happened. People started to creep, ever so tentatively and timidly, from the edges of the yard next door, then into the yard of the house where we stood. They reminded me of people emerging from air raid shelters after the bombings of London during World War II.

It turned out that these were the neighbors of the Korean gentleman who owned Baby. This neighborhood did not allow fences between adjacent yards, and they had not gone into their own yard for more than a year out of terror of this dog. Kent and I had liberated them. I was hoping for a ticker tape parade down the streets of Paris, or at least a gift certificate to Applebee's, but all I got were some bruises on my (unbroken) arm. Hardly a fair deal for freeing the world from Chowzilla.

CHAPTER TWENTY-THREE

The Illustrated Man

In Kent's third year out of school, we had two students working with us: Rick and Christina. One day, we got a call from a man who wanted Kent to do surgery on his ocelot. It's not that simple: the first thing Kent had to do was blood work and a physical to make sure it was safe to give the cat anesthesia. The man said OK and told us he was picking up the animal in Miami.

A couple of days later, this guy showed up at the clinic. This was the Illustrated Man. He had tattoos over 100% of his body that we could see (I don't want to speculate about the parts we couldn't see). Unfortunately, he strangely refused to have the cat's blood work done for some reason. Kent was firm: no blood work, no surgery. He wasn't going to be held liable for the death of an animal because the owner wouldn't let him follow correct procedure. But later, a kid came running in, yelling, "You gotta come quick, the ocelot is dying!" Kent didn't own the practice, so another vet went around him and did the surgery anyway, and the ocelot died. But that was only the beginning of the strangeness.

One of the things I've learned in working in our clinics is that you can never predict what people will do while they are alone in the examination room. We used to joke around about the weird stuff people did in the room when we weren't there. They might be making out or even having sex; you never knew. Well, while the ocelot was going to sleep under the anesthesia, the owner was having his picture taken with it. They didn't even get to the surgery! The thing expired before they could ever make an incision.

Chris Hill, who is now an executive at Hill's (the pet food company that makes Science Diet), was just a veterinary student at the time. Kent told Chris to go into the waiting room and take the patient history from the Illustrated Man. So Chris rushed in there. The owner was obviously gay and very weird, and the vet that put the animal to sleep had washed his hands of the whole thing, leaving Kent to clean up the mess.

Well, when Chris told the owner that his ocelot had, in the immortal words of John Cleese, "rung down the curtains and joined the choir invisible," the Illustrated Man broke into tears and threatened to kill everyone in the clinic with a shotgun. Kent went in the room to try and settle things down with a calm, "Let's talk about it" manner. He's very good at that sort of thing, which is helpful when you consider the oddballs who show up at the vet's office.

Meanwhile, back in Gotham City, the owner's lover showed up at the door. This chap (and I don't choose that word by accident) was a sight. He was resplendent in leather hot pants and a vest with no shirt. Vinnie (the boyfriend's name) was keeping it together pretty well—until the Illustrated Man confessed that he loved the ocelot more than he loved Vinnie. I really, really don't want to know if he meant "loved" literally.

So now Kent had two distraught, sobbing queens in the exam room. Veterinary school did not prepare him for this. He told them that he didn't own the practice and didn't do the surgery, but that he was going to make things right if they would give him some time. *How the fuck are you going to do that, Kent? I thought.* Resurrect the dead and create a cat zombie?

The sobbing lovers gave him 24 hours, and during that time they kept calling and threatening to come in and shoot everyone in the clinic, patients and doctors alike. I don't know why no one called the police. It may have been that it just didn't occur to anybody, but I think it was actually a perverse desire to see how the whole Gothic drama would play out, and law enforcement would inevitably have interfered with that.

So the 24 hours passed. There was a bar next door to our clinic, and Kent had never been to a bar in Florida, so he called the Drama Queens and said, "Why don't we just meet over there?" Yes, dear reader, you can see where this is going from a mile off. Kent went next door and there wasn't a light on anywhere, but there was a permanent installation of barflies in various stages of wretched intoxication. Into this gritty scene walk The Illustrated Man, Vinnie in his leathers, and my dear hubby in his white lab coat. Kent comes from a very sheltered background where people of one hue were on one side of the tracks and everyone else was on the other side. There were certainly no leather-clad gay bikers in his neighborhood growing up. But he gamely sat there and told them that the clinic's insurance company would take care of everything.

Eventually, the insurance company did just that. And as a result of that tense incident, we're a lot stricter about security. Today, if you threaten to kill everybody in one of our clinics with a shotgun, there's at least a 50-50 chance we're going to call the cops on you. So watch it.

CHAPTER TWENTY-FOUR

The High Life

When Kent was in veterinary school, class started at 7 a.m. All the students took turns bringing in donuts to go with the coffee. There were about 10 students in the class and everyone brought something. But one guy, named Burt, refused to bring snacks. Weeks went by and the other students razzed Burt until one day he caved in and brought in a plate of brownies. As Kent says, "They were amazing! I ate more than my share. Then, afterwards I had to go down and see patients."

It just so happened that there were 1,800 dogs in town for a regional dog show, and Kent had to care for some of them. So he went in to see one dog and take its temperature and history. He told me the story like this: "I got the information, and then went to write it down and then couldn't remember it. I did the same thing three times!" Yes, you've already figured it out, but Kent was from a conservative Midwest background, so you have to give him time to catch on.

He got some funny looks from the breeders, and then he decided to step outside to clear his head. Burt was out there, and Kent told Burt, "I think there's a gas leak, because my head is all cloudy." Burt broke up laughing hysterically, took one look at Kent's eyes and pronounced him very, very stoned. He'd added marijuana to the brownies! That was why he hadn't brought snacks to class; his munchies only gave you the munchies! But he'd had enough of being given a hard time by his fellow students and gave them a "be careful what you wish for" moment.

Kent and Burt and a few other students broke away from the dog show duty immediately to go upstairs and see if there were any more brownies left. Thank God, there were. They each ate another or two and then went back down. They were having a good old time, each of them more stoned than he had ever been (or in some cases, the first time he had been Rocky Mountain High), and some dog breeders got some very odd advice that morning.

Eventually, Kent and some other students headed down to radiology, where they were rotating around a set of x-rays and discussing them. It's a traditional way to learn. All was giggly and rather Beavis & Butthead-like until down came a professor to the radiology lab...carrying bags of chips and making a raft of ridiculous comments about the students, what they were wearing, and things that had nothing to do with medicine. Everyone but him knew he was stoned, and that was what made the situation pants-wettingly funny.

They were all laughing their asses off at the instructor, and the only question was who was more stoned, the students or the professor. Finally, one of the senior students, who was not part of the Brownie Posse and straight as an arrow, smelled a rat—a rat with an odor like an old tire burning. He became quite upset, went upstairs to the student lounge, took the last two brownies and walked them down to the toxicology lab to have them tested. He filled out the form and told the lab technician that he suspected that the brownies had marijuana in them. Understand, this would have been a serious violation of school codes if the students had been caught high as kites, and could have cost their professor his job. But no worries. As soon as the senior left, the tech ate the evidence. Case closed, and the tech had a really wonderful day eating everything in sight.

CHAPTER TWENTY-FIVE

Dr. Peck

Kent tells this one on his own: "Poultry medicine is a different animal, so to speak. They have farms with 500,000 birds on them. When one gets sick or some of them die, you have to bring in a sample of the birds, then the vets kill them and do autopsies to find out what's happening. It's quite brutal, and every vet-in-training has a turn at the wheel of the slaughterhouse. "Dr. Peck" (his real name was Dr. McClure) was in charge of poultry medicine at our school. He had a sour disposition, which I guess you would too if you spent your days smelling chicken shit and wringing necks.

"My favorite Dr. Peck story is about the time this guy showed up at the school with these chickens that he was proud of. He stopped by to get a health certificate on the way to a show. The receptionist directed him to "Dr. Peck", the only one there who was working on poultry at the time. 'What have you got?' barks Dr. Peck. Totally oblivious, the guy says, 'I got five chickens.' Well, Dr. Peck grabs them and before the guy can say a word, breaks their necks and lays them open on the dissection table. The guy that brought them in is just standing there with his mouth open. The doctor asks, 'What kind of losses are you having?' The poor man stammers, 'I just wanted a health certificate. I was going to show them!' Just another day at vet school.

"Dr. Peck smoked unfiltered Camels and he had this long, phlegmy cough with a moan attached to it. It was torture to listen to him hack up a lung like that, but two students at a time had to spend a week working with him and pretend he was important. I'm not sure why; maybe he had something on the chancellor or something."

Road Worrier

"My turn came one year, and when Dr. Peck coughed in front of me, I almost pissed myself laughing. I left the room to compose myself. At the end of the week we came in and asked what we would be doing for the day. He just sent us away. So we went up to the student lounge and got coffee and donuts. But now he came storming up the stairs and yelled at my partner until she was almost in tears. He really was an unstable guy, and I don't have a cue why he was allowed to practice veterinary medicine when he probably should have been spending his time in a clinical trial for antidepressants or something.

"Well, it turned out that Dr. Peck was angry because he needed to go to St. Louis to blood test and vaccinate a bunch of birds and he needed help. Guess who got drafted? So I sat between him and my weeping partner in the truck on the way to the city. On the dash of the truck was a huge file containing the records of these birds we were going up to see. Peck got in the truck and before he'd driven for ten minutes started yelling and screaming at me while he was driving. The man truly was off his chump. He was raving and ranting and swerving all over the road, hitting one concrete curb then the other. Meanwhile, when he wasn't watching me, I nudged Bev and smirked, just trying to get her to get her to lighten up, because she was really upset. The whole thing struck me as damned funny.

"So we're cruising along: Dr. Peck ranting, Bev sniffling, and me trying not to rupture something from suppressed laughter.

"We got on the interstate going 70 mph, and the wind caught the file on the dash and sent papers flying everywhere. I instinctively leaned down to pick them up, and Peck jabbed an elbow into my back. 'God damn it! I'll get them myself! Leave them alone!' he shouted. Of course, he was the one driving the truck, so gathering papers should not have been in his job description.

"I looked up and we were driving down the middle of the median and a bridge was coming up. 'Dr. McClure. Dr. McClure! We're driving in the median!' I shouted. At the last second, he swerved over, and I wasn't thinking this was so funny anymore. But was the crazy man contrite? Was he more careful?

"Hell, no. 'Better be glad I was driving the truck,' he snarled as poor Bev fought back a panic attack. 'Anyone else would've put us in the river!' The man was incredibly egotistical. My great hope is that one day a chicken just decided it had had enough and killed the son of a bitch."

CHAPTER TWENTY-SIX

Our Crazy Cat Lady

One Sunday, a lady came in with her big black cat. Obviously the cat was very ill; it was near the point of collapse, as was its owner. Kent wasn't at the office that day, so our associate vet, Kevin, was in charge. He told me we needed to take the cat back and draw some blood, run some tests and so on. All very routine. But this woman was having none of it. She refused to allow us to touch her cat until she'd read her tarot cards.

Kevin and I looked at each other and I was thinking that the crazy person quota for the week *had* seemed a little low. So out came the tarot cards and the woman feverishly laid them out and read them. I guess she found the Ace of Spayed or the Knight of Furballs or something favorable because she looked up and said, "You may attend to my cat." Gee, thanks, but in the few minutes that she was consulting her cards the cat had gotten considerably worse.

We examined the cat and discovered that it needed an immediate blood transfusion. We got permission to do a transfusion and we were back in the treatment area, busily trying to insert a catheter and draw blood from another cat, when in barged our crazy cat lady and began hitting poor

Kevin. Kevin was a young vet and a brilliant one, who graduated from veterinary school two years early. Kind of a Doogie Howser for animals. His specialty is cats; he would do anything to save them. We were lucky to have him.

Kevin was ducking haymakers that would have made Mike Tyson green with envy and all the while the woman was screaming, "Everyone knows you don't do a blood transfusion like that! Everyone knows you're just supposed to squirt blood in their mouths, you idiots!" Here poor Kevin had wasted all those years in veterinary school learning how to give blood transfusions the wrong way. Unfortunately, in the midst of the hitting and screaming and confusion, the poor cat expired.

Seeing this, Kevin tried to push this bizarre woman off him and perform CPR on the animal. But she grabbed the cat, announced that she would take him to be healed by Benny Hinn, the televangelist (who used to be based in the Orlando area and is now a mega-star in that world of the delusional and money-hungry), and dashed out the door, leaving Kevin and me and her $500 treatment bill behind.

Well. What does one say in the wake of something like that? In our case, one says, "Pay us." After all, there wasn't a lot we could do for the deceased cat, and if Benny Hinn did manage to resurrect it I'm sure we would have heard about it on the evening news. So we tried to track the woman down and get paid, figuring that was the end of our association with her. Not so.

About a week later, with Kent out of town, I got a very odd brown envelope in the mail. In it was a folder of the type that schoolchildren carry, covered with pictures of a cat and paw prints. I opened the folder with some trepidation, hoping that acid wouldn't shoot out of a hidden nozzle or something, and found a professionally taken photo of this tarot card woman posing in scanty lingerie. Suffice it to say this was a woman who had no business being in the same Zip code as a store selling such articles, much less wearing them. Behind the photo was a letter, handwritten in pencil on yellow-lined paper, so it looked like a letter home from the mental hospital:

"Hello mum, hello dad, talked to Napoleon today and he sends his best, banana carburetor fishing lure, sincerely, Robinson Crusoe."

Sighing something about being a weirdo magnet, I started reading the letter. She began by pointing out that her father had lived next to Lawton Chiles, who had been governor of Florida, and that her family was very important in the insurance industry, and that she had an IQ of 132.

Holy non sequitur, Batman! She mentioned that we should be able to see by the picture that she was very beautiful (ahem). Then we got to the meat of it: she wasn't so stupid that she didn't know that you were supposed to give blood transfusions orally, and how dare we ask for payment. Instead of paying us, she was going to sue us for the princely sum of $4,500. All I could think was, "Oh god, Kent, come home quickly."

Kent did come home and read the letter with a familiar, befuddled look on his face that said, "Four years of veterinary school for this?" Aside from being a wonderful husband and superb doctor, Kent is one hell of a letter writer. So he sat down and drafted our response to Ms. Crazy Cat Lady. He suggested that in the future, she should leave the occult to the tarot cards, the spiritual to the likes of Benny Hinn, and the medicine to the veterinarians, as long as she never set foot inside our clinic again, and by the way, she still owed us $500. Off this missive went in a cloud of stamp glue and a hearty cry of "Please seek psychiatric help!"

Another week later, we got a new envelope, this one featuring different handwriting used for each line of the address, like some sort of amateur attempt at code. Oh goody, I thought, more from our favorite loony, still successfully defending her title against all challengers. I wondered if I would end up like those children in the 1950s who would wait for the mailman to deliver the latest *Saturday Evening Post* because it contained the newest installment of a serial mystery. A note from my serial psychotic had arrived and I was giddy.

This letter started much the same way, rambling on about the governor of Florida and so on, and it ended with the comment that she would, and I quote, "rather be fucked by dykes in prison with a Coke bottle than ever come into your clinic again." At the bottom of the letter, she attached a P.S.: "I thought you should know your receptionist told me that you're sleeping with your associate veterinarian."

Always up for adding some spice to the workday, I called Kevin into my office and asked him to read the letter. I watched, straight-faced, as he moved down the letter and saw his eyes get big as the read the postscript. "Now Kevin," I said, "If you're sleeping with Kent, I think you should just tell me so I don't have to find out this way." We had a good laugh about that and I promised I wouldn't let Kent know that I knew about their torrid affair.

Kent has a favorite saying about our work: "You should always be careful about wrestling with pigs. You're going to get filthy and the pig's just going to enjoy it." Our brief but remarkably disturbed correspondence with the tarot card lady ended there, because we realized if we replied, she might never stop. But to this day, I occasionally find myself idling by the mailbox, waiting for another letter in that childlike penmanship. For one thing, it was about 98 degrees out when she stormed out of here with her dead cat, and it's easily an hour drive to Orlando. I want to know what the Reverend Hinn made of the smell.

ABOUT THE AUTHORS

Annie Greer is a certified veterinary chiropractioner, radio host, animal behaviorist, farmer's wife and AKC Canine Good Citizen evaluator who, with her veterinarian husband, Kent, runs three animal clinics in Apopka, Florida.

Tim Vandehey is a professional ghostwriter and book collaborator. Since 2004, he has collaborated on more than 30 books in the self-improvement, memoir, spiritual, health, business and financial genres, including *What If and Why Not* with Jen Groover (BenBella), *Red Carpet Ready* with Melissa Rivers (Harmony), *Blindsided* with Jim Cole (St. Martin's Press), and *Running on Faith* with Jason Lester (HarperOne). Tim lives on Bainbridge Island, Washington with his wife and two daughters.

www.ingramcontent.com/pod-product-compliance
Lightning Source LLC
Chambersburg PA
CBHW031641040426
42453CB00006B/179